D1391762

VULNERABLE IN HEARTS

Vulnerable in Hearts

a memoir of fathers, sons and contract bridge

SANDY BALFOUR

ATLANTIC
BOOKS

First published in Great Britain
in 2005 by Atlantic Books,
an imprint of Grove Atlantic Ltd.

Every effort has been made
to contact copyright holders.
The publishers will be pleased
to make good any omissions or
rectify any mistakes brought to
their attention at the earliest
opportunity.

9 8 7 6 5 4 3 2 1

A CIP catalogue record for
this book is available from the
British Library.

ISBN 1 84354 365 6

Printed in Great Britain by
MPG Books, Bodmin, Cornwall
Design by Lindsay Nash

Atlantic Books
An imprint of Grove Atlantic Ltd
Ormond House
26–27 Boswell Street
London WC1N 3JZ

for my brother

The sights and sounds of my youth pursue me;
and I see like a vision the youth of my father, and
of his father, and the whole stream of lives flowing
down there far in the north, with the sound of
laughter and tears ...

R.L. Stevenson, from the dedication to *Catriona*

Contents

PART IV A VALEDICTION FORBIDDING MOURNING

PART I

ONE DAY IN JANUARY

1. Shuffling

WE WERE A family of five, which is the perfect number for bridge. Four to play and one to make tea. I say 'were' because Dad is no longer with us. He died with a void in diamonds and a hole in his heart and, though I loved him dearly, I sometimes thought I hardly knew him. He died quietly and not quite alone in a hospital in Durban in the summer of 2003. He was angry and sad and he made me smile. When he laughed his whole body shook. It would start with his shoulders. They would heave up and down like a threshing machine. Then it would spread to his stomach and his cheeks. His jowls waggled like an old bulldog, while his bony knees knocked together like castanets. His laugh could fill a room or a hall or a young boy's world until a coughing fit caught up with him and he would turn puce and hawk and spit to clear

3

his throat of tobacco-stained phlegm. Even now people speak of it. It made us giggle and reduced him to tears.

I saw a lot of him in his last few days. He was in a hospital in Durban in a room that looked over the bay. There were container ships out to sea and a breeze in the trees. We talked a lot too, more than in the twenty years since I left South Africa. There was nothing else to do. He couldn't move, and I couldn't budge. I felt bolted to the chair beside his hospital bed and I spent the hours watching the life ebb and flow in his strange, depleted white body. Some days he was tired; others he seemed stronger. Our conversations were as they had always been, coded, cautious and full of silences. They were like the bidding in bridge. Few words were needed, and those we used took on different meanings depending on when they were said and by whom. He said dying was sad only for those who insist on living. He asked whether it was cold, or was it just him? He said he had nothing to say and that he wanted to shave. He wished his bloody hands would stop shaking.

I said I was sorry.

He said to give his regards to the kids – my kids, his grand-children.

'Just regards?' I asked.

'Aye,' he said. 'The rest they'll get from you.'

I wondered what the rest was. When I asked if he had any regrets, he made what in bridge is sometimes called a 'forcing pass'. It required a response from his partner, although exactly what this response should be would have depended on the partnership understanding and on what the others at the table might have to say for themselves. Often a forcing pass comes into play when one or other pair at the bridge table is about to or has the opportunity to make a 'sacrifice bid'. A sacrifice bid means that the partnership reaches a contract which it knows it is unlikely to succeed in making, but which it anticipates will be less expensive than allowing the opponents to make a rival contract. The scoring in bridge works that way. If you make a vulnerable contract of four spades, it's worth 620 points to you. And nothing to your opponents. If they're not vulnerable, they might decide to bid five clubs even though they know they're unlikely to make it. Because, even if they fall three short of the required number of tricks, it will cost them only 150 points. They lose – but, relatively speaking, they win. Partners playing the forcing pass sometimes have to guess. Should I bid or shouldn't I? And, if so, what? I knew that I would have to decide the question of Dad's regrets for myself.

At least he was glad to hear I was playing bridge again. He thought it would do me good. He'd been playing a bit with a bunch of grumpy old men from the local club. Each afternoon they would meet in a different house. Their wives would put out sandwiches and tea and go to the movies. But they'd play in silence and it wasn't much fun. In the last couple of years, he had more or less given it up. Pity, in a way, but what could you do? If it wasn't fun, there wasn't much point, not even to keep Alzheimer's at bay.

'Do you remember actually learning the game?' I asked.

'No, not in any detail.'

Detail was important to Dad. He liked things to be precise. He liked mathematics.

'Everyone has to learn somewhere,' I suggested.

'Sure,' he said, shrugging.

I told him I had read somewhere a story about Omar Sharif. Sharif is almost as famous for his bridge as he is for his movies. In one interview, he said that he learned bridge while relaxing on a movie set in Egypt in 1954. 'I found myself with a lot of spare time waiting for the cameras to be ready. I found a dusty old book and read it. It happened to be about bridge. Had it been about fishing or gardening, I would have been a healthier, outdoor, tanned old man,' he said.

Dad supposed he had learned bridge from his parents back when they lived in Edinburgh. Come to think of it, he was sure he had.

'It would have been Pa that taught me,' he said, 'although Ma wasn't so bad herself.'

'A bit like you and Mum,' I suggested.

But Dad was lost in a reverie that sped him back across the decades to Edinburgh. That's where he grew up, in a house on a hill in the south of the city. This was in the late thirties, when bridge was at its most popular. His dad was a bank clerk and his mother a teacher. It would have been strange if they hadn't taught him bridge.

'Aye, but it was Uncle Willie made me love it,' he said.

Dad remembered that his uncle Willie played until old age. He had lived in the Borders someplace, in Scotland, and suffered from Parkinson's disease. His eyes shone and his hands shook. When he came to stay they would play through the night. Willie had been gassed in the trenches during the Great War. Dad said he kept everyone awake with his coughing. The next morning he'd put them to sleep with his analysis of the play. When he could no longer keep thirteen cards in his hands, his brothers built a special wooden rack to hold them.

I wondered what happened to the rack. Dad asked why it mattered. I said because things do and he said perhaps. He said it was a pity we couldn't play. He would have liked to beat me one more time.

'But we always played together,' I whispered.

'Och, aye,' he said. 'Boys against girls.' He and I were the 'boys'. My mother and sister, Jackie, were the 'girls'. Sometimes thinking (erroneously, as it happens) that I was better than Jackie (and certain, it goes without saying, that he was better than Mum), Dad would mix us up a little, which is to say I would play with Mum and he with Jackie. But this arrangement never quite worked. There was no edge to it and we all played worse as a result. The former plan was better. They may have got all the points, but we got all the glory, and in Dad's mind the pursuit of points was as nothing compared to the pursuit of glory.

'So how could you beat me?' I asked. 'We were partners.'

But he passed again, which was my punishment for being too bloody literal. And, besides, it is not unknown at the bridge table for players to treat their partners even more brutally than their opponents. Zia Mahmood, one of the great players of the modern generation, writes (approvingly, by the way) of a particular player who frequents the New York bridge club scene and who 'played what I call "Israeli Savage", an aggressive version of "Paki Savage". Basically, the system has two rules: 1) Bid no trump and 2) punish your partner and your opponents alike without mercy.' Mahmood comes from Pakistan, though he now plays for the United States, and is a keen advocate of what he calls 'Paki Savage', an unbridled style of bidding intended to make life extremely difficult for your opponents. And if your partner can't keep up? Well, that's his problem.

Dad smiled at my discomfort, which must have hurt like hell. He wanted to laugh but his body couldn't take it. Even the smallest movement pulled at the stitches from the operation to clear the cancerous blockage in his throat. He winced and closed his eyes, which was how he disguised his pain. I could see he was drifting off. It was time to go. He held my hand a moment.

'You can still play,' he said. 'You'll have David.'

David is my elder brother.

'He doesn't play,' I said. 'He doesn't like the game.'

'Och, *ja*, so he says.' My father is the only person I have known to say *ja* with an Edinburgh lilt.

'It's true, he doesn't.'

David is a scientist, a botanist and an ecologist. For many years he has lived and worked in South Africa's game reserves. His fingers are scarred from working in the bush. He is tall, tanned and muscular. There is rhino dung under his nails and he smells vaguely of diesel. He doesn't look like a bridge player and he doesn't want to be one. If he were on a movie set and found a book about bridge, he would use it to prop up his wobbly workbench. Despite his upbringing, despite his father, despite *everything,* David has never shown any interest in bridge. Not a glimmer. Once, when asked to play, he said he would rather bathe in soggy lettuce, a vegetable to which he at that time had a near-pathological aversion.

'Everyone likes bridge,' Dad said. 'They just don't know it yet.'

2. Brothers-in-arms

DAVID DOESN'T EAT meat and I don't drink alcohol, but this morning we're doing both. Beyond the bougainvillea-laden fringe of the veranda where we sit, the sun drips on to a dappled lawn. There have been night rains and the air is clean and fresh and for the moment it is almost cool. There is enough cloud to suggest that it might rain again, but for now tendrils of steam rise from the leaves and grass and a slight breeze caresses the leaves of the jacaranda trees that line the driveway. A cat stretches out on the windowsill.

We've gone for the works. 'Everything,' David said to the waiter. 'Eggs, bacon, sausage, mushroom, beans, maybe a bit of steak? Toast, hash browns, I don't know. Bring us everything you've got. Maybe put some cheese on that steak.'

'And champagne,' I added. 'Your most expensive. And orange juice and coffee and maybe a little fruit salad.'

'With ice cream,' says David.

The waiter looks at us and starts from the top.

'Eggs for two?'

'Please.'

'Scrambled or fried?'

'Scrambled,' I say. David prefers his fried.

'And sausage?'

'*Ja.*'

'Also for two.'

We're laughing now and the waiter is beginning to relax a little. After all, it is late for breakfast, a little after eleven in the morning, and we are the only customers in the restaurant.

'Mushroom, beans, toast, steak. Everything,' David says.

'And champagne,' I repeat.

'The most expensive?' says the waiter with the trace of a grin.

'You got it. Two bottles.'

'Two bottles?' He looks at me and then slowly begins to write. '2 btle Chmp.'

'But don't open them, OK. I think *we* should open them. And cold please.' I turn to my brother. 'I can't drink the stuff unless it's really cold.'

'OK,' says the waiter. He looks at the list on his pad. 'You want the fruit salad first or last.'

'Together,' says David. 'Except the champagne. We want that first.'

'And maybe the ice cream. Bring the ice cream and the champagne first.'

Eventually the waiter is confident that he has our order. As he disappears through the large French doors that open on to the veranda where we're sitting, he casts one last backward glance at us as if he thinks we might make a run for it the moment he is out of sight. There's something not quite right about these two middle-aged men behaving like schoolboys at this hour of the morning. And so well dressed?

It doesn't add up, but it's true. We are well dressed. I'm wearing a suit and dark tie, and a new white shirt. The gleam of my polished shoes mirrors my shiny face because for once I am freshly shaven. David, of course, isn't. It must be twenty years since he was last clean-shaven and probably longer since he last wore a tie. But by his standards he looks quite respectable. His cotton shirt is neatly pressed and his trousers have a crease. He has even polished his shoes. He got married a decade ago, so maybe it's only ten years since he last polished his shoes.

We look at each other; there is not much to say, but slowly the hint of a smile begins to form around the corner of his mouth, and I can feel mine starting too. Once we start to giggle, there's no stopping us. Holding our sides, lying face down on the table, we laugh until we cry, and then we laugh some more. Our shoulders shake, but only moderately.

'Oh, Christ,' I say, 'the porn!'

'Jesus, I'll never forget those bloody pictures. Did you see Mum's face?'

'And the handprints on the wall? Must have been ash!'

And we laugh again at the thought of Mum's face, and the porn and the handprints of the ashes of the dead on the wall, even though the porn wasn't hardcore, just the centrefolds from *Scope* magazine, South Africa's equivalent of 'Page Three Girls'.

'Oh, dear God.'

But after a while the laughter can't sustain itself, and we sit up a little straighter and look back to the French doors.

'I hope I never have to do that again,' I say.

'You won't,' says David.

It takes me a moment to work out the truth of this statement. Just then the woman who owns the restaurant comes through the French doors. She is carrying a silver tray with a bottle of champagne, a carafe of orange juice and two bowls of vanilla ice cream.

'So *howzit*, gents?' she says in a South African accent so strong that if I had heard it in London it would have sent shivers down my spine. But here in Hillcrest, KwaZulu-Natal, on this warm summer's day with a hoopoe on the lawn and a purple-crested loerie in the avocado tree, it sounds just about right. It is warm and throaty, filled with the sound of sun and cigarettes and the evening *dop*. 'What's the celebration?'

David is busy with the champagne bottle and so it falls to me to answer. 'You don't want to know,' I say.

'Ah, come on,' she replies, 'don't keep it to yourselves.'

She's maybe our age, maybe a little older, maybe quite a bit older, when I look too closely. I guess she's fifty, which makes her ten years older than me, seven more than David. She's not unattractive, here in the subdued light of a cool veranda in a quiet commuter suburb twenty miles inland from Durban. She's wearing a loose terracotta skirt and a white blouse. Her eyes are blue and her hair – for today at least – is auburn. It's not hard to imagine her story. The marriage, the kids, the divorce. No doubt the divorce was delayed long enough for the kids to grow up, go to university, leave home. Then came the settlement that meant she could buy the restaurant. Her finger has the shadow of a ring. Perhaps she took it off for us.

She eyes us up and begins to flirt a little. I notice that she is even in her favours. Neither of us wears a ring. Perhaps she's wondering which of us is older because, although I look it, David has a quiet authority about him. And anyway he's better looking than me, despite the beard. Without it, he looks a lot like Dad. He has the same long, thin face and deep-set eyes, the same high cheekbones and caterpillar eyebrows. They're both tall and thin, although David is not exceptionally so. Unlike Dad, he can stand against a window and still be seen. Light doesn't refract around him.

'You look a lot like him,' I say.

'It could be worse,' he says. 'I could sound like him.'

'Like you,' he adds, in case I've missed the point. The cork pops and David pours the champagne.

'You'd better get yourself a glass,' I say to the owner.

At first she demurs. 'It's your party, gents. Enjoy.' But under a little pressure she begins to relent. There's some bargaining to be done first. 'I need to know what I'm drinking to,' she says, as she sends the waiter off to fetch another champagne flute and takes a seat at our table.

David pours her champagne and we solemnly raise our glasses.

'To Dad,' I say.

'Dad,' David repeats.

'It's his birthday?' she asks.

I'm shaking my head as we drink. 'Uh, uh. His funeral.'

3. Voices

DAD'S FUNERAL WAS a simple affair, just the close family and no priest. By the time we came to say goodbye to him, he had moved sufficiently far away from the Catholic Church for the service to be ignored altogether. No Mass. No last rites. No repentance. None of 'that', at Dad's request and to our considerable relief, although in fact he put it more strongly. Instead, we make it up, not quite as we go along. David says a few words. Mum reads John Donne's *A Valediction Forbidding Mourning*. She must have nerves of steel for there is not the hint of a quiver in her voice. My sister Jackie prefers to say nothing.

We're in the chapel of a cemetery on the outskirts of Durban. It's a beautiful place, several acres of rolling hills surrounded by frangipani and jacaranda, erythrina and mango trees. While Mum speaks, I start to read the memorial plaques around the walls of the chapel. There are perhaps 200 of them. Robert Louis Stevenson's *Requiem* is quoted no less than eight times, and I study the names on these plaques. MacLean, Borthwick, Lee. Scots, all of them, who had come this far and died here, 10,000 miles from 'the auld country', and I'm willing to bet every last one of them 'wearied', as Dad sometimes claimed to, 'for the heather' and the 'green Highland hills of home'.

Then it's my turn and, while the others gaze silently at the coffin or the ceiling or their feet, I stumble through the *Requiem*:

> Under the wide and starry sky
> Dig the grave and let me lie:
> Glad did I live and gladly die,
> And I laid me down with a will.

> This be the verse you 'grave for me:

It's the sixth line that gets me. Up to that point, I just about manage to hold it together and to obey Donne's injunction:

> ... let us melt, and make no noise,
> No tear-floods, nor sigh-tempests move ...

I'm reciting the *Requiem* from memory and, as line follows line, I realise that Dad must have taught us the words before my memories begin. Not once have I lain beneath the wide and starry sky anywhere in the world but that the lines have come back to me. The hunter is home, he would announce, coming in from the office. I gladly die, he would say at the bridge table before making a sacrifice bid of 5 ♣ and thereby robbing our opponents of their rightful game in 4 ♠. And sometimes, *apropos* nothing in particular, he would recite the poem in its entirety and his voice would take on a slightly stronger brogue while his grey eyes misted over. And it wasn't just the *Requiem*, but the entire Stevenson canon. In the restless forests of his life, *A Child's Garden of Verses* was a constant and we might at any moment expect to hear a favourite line or stanza or entire poem quoted without context, except that the context was his life, and who he was. He liked the rhythm of Stevenson's poetry and the journeys. He was much more interested in the journey than in arriving, though it is only now that I see it in the poems he used to recite from *A Child's Garden of Verses*.

> Dark brown is the river
> Golden is the sand.
> It flows along forever,
> With trees on either hand...

In the poem, the child narrating it builds boats and sets them afloat on the river, and watches them go out of sight, 'away past the mill'. And my father's eyes would cloud a little at the concluding line:

> Other little children
> Shall bring my boards ashore.

He also loved the rhythms of 'From a Railway Carriage' with its

> ... child who clambers and scrambles,
> All by himself and gathering brambles;
> Here is a tramp who stands and gazes;
> And here is the green for stringing the daisies!
> Here is a cart runaway in the road
> Lumping along with man and load;
> And here is a mill, and there is a river:
> Each a glimpse and gone forever!

Dad's life has been full of such glimpses.

When it came to the funeral, I knew there was only one tribute I could pay. The *Requiem* continues,

Here he lies where he long'd to be ...

But, at the thought of Dad's longing, my voice breaks. Tears well up and I lose it completely. I stand, unable to speak or move, wracked by wave after wave of sobbing. I have one hand on the coffin. I'm sure that if I lift it I will fall over. I wonder what one does when one can't speak, and can't move and everybody's watching. Does it stay like this forever?

It doesn't. The spell breaks and I manage to blunder my way through the last three lines, thinking all the while that it was perfectly possible that none of them was true:

> Here he lies where he long'd to be;
> Home is the sailor, home from the sea,
> And the hunter home from the hill.

And then it is time for the coffin to be taken through the doors at the back of the chapel to the crematorium. To the funeral director's surprise, we have said we will carry the coffin to the furnace ourselves. I don't know why; perhaps we wanted to prolong the moment of parting. Perhaps we are just being Balfours, which is to say we are copying Dad's perennial insistence on doing every last bloody thing ourselves. He was the declarer and he played the hand. The rest could do as they wished.

David, Jackie and I push the trolley through. Mum follows behind, as we go through some heavy curtains, not knowing quite what to expect. We enter a room the size of a squash court. In the middle is a large oven. There are no windows and only a pale neon light illuminates the room. Around the side are a few bare tables and chairs. And in the corner a shovel. The pillars near the door are marked with handprints of grey ash. And seated at the table are the men whose job it is normally to take the coffin and shove it into the oven. They're leafing through *Scope* and *Hustler* and they have put up centrefolds on the walls, silent witnesses no doubt to their daily rota of cremations. They stand up when we come in, but the funeral director motions to them to stand back and they let us do it ourselves. One of them picks up his magazine from where he dropped it on the floor and resumes his reading, if reading is what he was doing.

It is only later that we find this funny. For the moment, we concentrate on the furnace. It is big and dark and has a little glass panel through which one can see whatever goes on inside. A small blue pilot light hisses softly. David and I heave the coffin in. We close the door with a bright metallic clang and look to the funeral director. He indicates a dial on one side of the oven.

'All the way?' David asks.

He nods. 'You want it good and hot.'

While I wonder what it is, exactly, that I want, David turns the dial. Through the glass panel on the door we watch the blue flames begin to lap the sides of Dad's coffin. And even in that broad daylight on a summer's day in Durban, I feel the sky growing darker yet and the sea ever higher.

As we turn to leave, I feel the eyes of naked women follow me across the room.

There are matters to be attended to for the memorial event that afternoon. Catering must be arranged, phone calls made. Mum and Jackie will head home. David and I have to fetch a few things from Hillcrest. We're on the way there when we decide to stop for breakfast.

'Thank God it's over,' I say, but David's not sure it ever will be.

That evening, Mum is on the phone for the umpteenth time talking to another friend. I listen to her side of the conversation.

'Yes, on Tuesday... Yes, I'm sure... Oh, no, I'll be fine... Yes, Jackie's here, and the boys too...'

I've flown in from London, Jackie from Brussels. David lives and works in a game reserve three hours' drive away. At the memorial event that afternoon, friends of my parents whom I haven't seen for twenty or thirty years peer myopically at me.

'Now which one are you, dear?' they ask.

'I'm Sandy.'

'My, haven't you grown...'

But their voices invariably trail off and I never know how the sentence will end. Bald? Fat? Just like your father, who was neither of those things?

And Mum's holding it together pretty well, quietly answering the same questions over and over. 'No, there was some pain... Yes, the drugs helped... Yes, completely, 'til the very end.'

This last comment refers to Dad's mind, which, unlike his body, was in pretty good shape when he died.

In the early afternoon, I head back to the crematorium to pick up Dad's ashes. The funeral director is expecting me. He has a cardboard box on his desk. It's labelled neatly 'Mr Balfour'.

'It doesn't look like me,' I say.

'Sign here,' says the director.

I sign and then pick up the box. It's still warm.

'Busy day?' I ask.

The director chooses not to reply. I can tell from his face that he has learned under these circumstances that it is better to say nothing.

'Thank you,' I say.

My parents live in a house on a hill in a suburb near Durban. On clear days, it is possible to see the Indian Ocean to the east. To the west lie rolling hills covered with well-tended trees and large houses on acre and half-acre plots. The garden at our house slopes away to either side. In the front is a main lawn, a vast expanse of grass, the centrepiece of which is an old flat crown tree. It is very big, the biggest I've ever seen. We spread Dad's ashes there just as dark falls.

Dad loved the tree and it reminds me of him. Its branches spread out above the lawn reaching from one side of the garden to the other. In full leaf it provides perhaps half an acre of shade. It takes in the lawn and the strawberry beds, the banks above what used to be the tennis court and the flowerbeds. It has a huge, thick, smooth grey trunk and flat overarching branches, which stretch out magnificently like some kind of *Angel of the South*. Below it other plants flourish. This is high summer and the garden looks particularly good. The lawn is green and the azalea is in bloom. The avocado tree is laden with fruit. And the tree has other uses. For as long as I can remember, the monkeys that live in our part of South Africa have used it as a highway from one side of our property to the other. We used to shoot them with the pellet gun in the vain hope that they would eat the neighbours' fruit instead of ours. The bark of the trunk is pockmarked with pellet scars from where we used to do target practice as kids. Near the base around the back, I find my name half-scratched in the bark. I must have been twelve when I found a sharp knife and started to carve, but I never got beyond the 'A'. Dad stopped me with a shake of his head. 'There are better ways to make your mark,' he said. 'Let the tree grow.'

As darkness falls, the last guests leave and the telephone stops ringing. Quiet settles on the old house. The four of us gather in the sitting room, unsure what to do or say. Instead, we listen to the sounds of the suburbs. Dogs bark. From across the valley the sounds of a party are carried on the night breeze. A thousand frogs croak. I am struck, and not for the first time, by how comically precarious the suburbs appear to be. For all their appearance of solidity, one has only to witness the extraordinary scale of work that is required to keep 'the bush' at bay, the gardeners and lawn-mowers, chemicals, irrigation systems, planting, pruning, hoeing and weeding, to know that should the people disappear it would take only a few years, months even, for the bush to reclaim these immaculate lawns with their swimming pools and herbaceous borders, their tennis courts and arbours. Our property is large and the house too far from the roads for us to hear the traffic, but we can hear the trees creak in the breeze. Every now and then, the old house seems to sigh.

Ours is the kind of household in which a pack of cards is always near to hand. I find myself staring blankly at one such pack on the table in front of me.

'We could always play bridge?' I say. But no one takes me up on the offer. They don't think it's true any more.

PART II

WHEN MY WORLD WAS YOUNG

4. Walking on the moon

LET ME TAKE you back.

It is the South African winter of 1969. I am seven years old and I do not yet know that I like bridge. In other areas, I have learned to discriminate, which means that, while some things impress me, others do not. I do not, for example, think much of the neighbour's dog, which barks and dribbles. But I am impressed that every morning the postman cycles up the hill to deliver our letters. He wears a grey uniform and has a drooping moustache. One side is slightly longer than the other. At the back door, my mother offers him a glass of orange squash, which he drinks gratefully.

'Thank you,' he says. Beads of sweat form on his brow. He wipes them aside and replaces his cap. I run to the garden gate to watch him cycle away. As he starts to descend the hill, he lets go of the handlebars. I envy the way the wind lifts his shirt.

'When I'm big,' I say, 'I'm going to be a postman.'

My mother smiles indulgently. 'I don't think you can,' she says absently. 'It's a job for Indians.'

It is many years before I work out what this means. But in 1969 the realities of apartheid do not impinge on my life. Following the massacre at Sharpeville and the banning of the African National Congress, the Communist Party and other organisations, the apartheid state appears to be all-powerful. Some have referred to this period (with appropriate irony) as 'the golden age of apartheid'. The economy is booming and South Africa's white population is its beneficiary. Those who resisted white rule have been banned, killed or imprisoned. The Black Consciousness Movement has not yet taken shape. Organised labour is anything but and the African National Congress is underground or in exile. It is down but not out. Nelson Mandela and his colleagues are six or seven years into their long prison sentences on Robben Island. While they are on the island, several of them spend many hours playing bridge. So does the man who will one day set them free. South Africa's future president and Nobel Peace Laureate F.W. de Klerk is also an avid bridge player and has been since he was a child.

We live in a modest house with a large garden in a suburb of Pietermaritzburg, a small market town sometimes known as 'sleepy hollow'. It developed delusions of grandeur once it, and not Durban, was made the capital of what was then Natal Province in the newly reconstituted Union of South Africa. The author Tom Sharpe lived there for a time until he was deported for sins against the apartheid government. Back in England he went on to write his bawdy satires of life in 'Piemburg'. He called them *Riotous Assembly* and *Indecent Exposure*, both of which were considered crimes by the humourless autocrats in Pretoria. In Sharpe's books, the wealthy English-speaking class of Pietermaritzburg are lampooned with a variable degree of accuracy as subsisting on a diet of murder, alcohol and sex. The town itself was 'built in the heyday of the British Empire' and the 'tiny metropolis still possessed an air of seedy grandeur. The City Hall, redbrick Gothic, loomed above the market square while, opposite, the Supreme Court maintained a classical formal air.' Ripley's *Believe it or Not!*, which adorns the back of the wrappers of a popular brand of chewing gum, tells me that Pietermaritzburg City Hall is the largest redbrick building in the southern hemisphere. Of such modest claims is Pietermaritzburg made. It is here that my father works as a chemical engineer, while my mother raises the children and gives French lessons to private pupils.

In the evenings we read books or listen to the radio. I remember, for example, the day Neil Armstrong walked on the moon. South Africa would not have a television service for another seven years and my father was listening to it on the radio, brought to us by 'the BBC in London', wherever that might be. The radio sat in the corner of the sitting room. It was an old 'valve' wireless that hissed and spat as it warmed up. In the gathering gloom of winter evenings, my father would turn it on to listen on weekdays to what he called 'his sums', which was actually the stock market report, and on weekends to 'Music in the Blue of Eve', a classics compilation brought to us by the 'English' Service of Radio South Africa. This was his staple fare, but from time to time we would tune in to the World Service of the BBC. It was on the World Service that we listened to the first moon landings.

'You'll remember this for the rest of your life,' Dad said. I remember wondering if this was true. For a start, the 'rest of my life' seemed impossibly distant. I could no more imagine being forty-two (his age then; my age as I write this) than I could imagine 'London' or 'the BBC'. And, secondly, walking on the moon did not seem that big a deal. Only that afternoon I had personally paddled across the Amazon in a cardboard box, making landfall beneath the plum tree at the bottom of the garden just as night fell. Neither the boa constrictors nor the best efforts of a

34

tribe of Indians could stop me and I had just enough time to beach my craft and disguise it with twigs before going in for supper.

Dad is lost in wonder at the moon landings, and not only because Neil Armstrong's roots are in the same part of the Scottish Borders as his. His eyes are moist as he gazes into the distance. From time to time, he shakes his head at the miracles that science has made possible. Together we stand on the lawn and gaze into the twinkling night. The moon is a thin sliver in the sky over Pietermaritzburg.

'They're up there now. Can you imagine that? Walking on the moon. That must be as good as it gets,' he says. 'No one can ever trump that.'

This does not overly impress me. I have little doubt that one day I will walk on the moon, possibly on my way to Mars. Instead, I focus on the new word. 'What does "trump" mean?' I ask.

A slow grin spreads over Dad's face. 'This ought to be fun,' he says. 'Go and fetch your brother.'

But David is busy softening up a rabbit skin. I never find out where they come from, but at that time it is not unusual to find rabbit skins pegged out in the back garden. Dad brings tannin home from work so David can cure them. To my surprise, he seems to like doing this. He arranges the pelts neatly in rows and tells me not to worry about the blood. He shows me where their eyes were and how the membrane peels off easily if only I will do it right.

'We're all like that under the skin,' he says.

I leave him to his gore and go inside to recruit my sister, Jackie. Together she and I will learn about this new word, 'trump'.

Dad sits us round the table. 'Right,' he says, 'I'm going to teach you how to play bridge.'

It seems entirely reasonable that to understand a word we must first learn a game. But it is not until I teach my children how to play bridge that I see that the first thing they understand is the idea of trumps.

It is April 2003, a couple of months after Dad died. April is South Africa's autumn, and my girlfriend and I and our three children are in the Drakensberg mountains, where we have rented a holiday cottage.

The weather is kind to us. The days are hot and we spend them walking mountain trails and swimming in fledgling streams. When my brother joins us for a few days, we go rock climbing. He finds his way to the top of the cliff so that he can belay the children from above while I stand below and offer helpful advice.

'Move your left foot across to that toehold. No, not that left foot, the other one.'

My girlfriend is nervous of heights. She likes the idea of our children climbing cliffs, but she does not like to watch. She takes photographs with her eyes shut.

In the cold evenings, we barbecue chops and *boerewors* and watch the mountain air darken. My son, Cal, is eight years old. He likes to play with the hot coals. He pushes them from one side of the barbecue pit to the other. He lights sticks and holds them up against the darkness.

'To keep the baboons away,' he says, with only a passing regard for the truth.

The nights fall swiftly at this time of year and soon we find ourselves retreating into the warmth of the cottage. One evening, I get out a pack of cards. 'Come on,' I say, 'I'll show you how to play bridge.'

My brother snorts loudly. Neither he nor my girlfriend is interested in playing, but the children are keen. They like games. We settle round the table to play, as always, boys against girls. Cal and me against my two daughters. The girls look forward to beating us. We 'boys' put on a wholly unjustified air of nonchalant superiority. I deal the first hand and start to run through the basics.

'You need to understand that the idea of the game is first to reach a "contract" by agreeing how many "tricks" your partnership will make,' I say. 'And then you need to try to make them. A trick is a round of four cards, with one card being played in turn by each player.' And even in saying this I knew that the phrases were not mine but my father's and that my voice was my father's voice. 'There are fifty-two cards in the pack and there are therefore thirteen tricks to be won. Got that? Fifty-two divided by four is thirteen. The highest card of the suit played first wins the trick. Unless it is trumped. In agreeing the number of tricks your partnership will try to make, you are also determining which suit will be "trumps". Trumps are cards with special powers. If a trump card is played on a non-trump lead, the trump wins the trick.'

It is only in watching my own children that I realise that it is trumps that first hold a child's attention. Children love the idea that a little baby of a card like the two of whatever suit is trumps can silence a big adult ace of something else. Trumps upset the adult order of things. They invert the natural hierarchy. Trumps make the weak strong and the strong weak. They have miraculous properties. They are biblical, like floods and plagues. There is a violence to trumps, which can take the highest card and spit in its face. They are David to Goliath. But there is a gentility to them too. Trumps can turn water into wine. With them, the meek can inherit the earth.

At this point I no longer sound like my father. In the good Catholic household of *my* childhood such flippant views were not

expressed. But they were understood. The meek and their place –
if we take 'meek' to mean the disempowered majority – were, of
course, a subject of some concern. Repression cannot last forever.
In South Africa, the numbers alone meant that the apartheid government could not endure forever. And, though for the moment
'things were quiet', nobody could be confident that it would
always be this way. This also was not discussed in our good
Catholic household.

What is discussed are the magical properties of trumps.

'There's many a man,' my father says, 'who walked the streets
of London because he didn't draw trumps.' Assuming the bidding
has not been stupid, the declarer – the person playing the hand –
will have more trumps than his opponents. It is often, though
not always, in his interest to force the opponents to play their
trumps (i.e. to 'draw' them) so that the only ones remaining are
his own. Otherwise, he is likely to find himself losing tricks he
thought he would win and failing to make contracts that would
otherwise have been 'cold'. Cold, in bridge, means 'certain to
succeed'. From failing to make cold contracts, it is only a short
step out on to the cold streets. 'Cold' in this sense means something completely different. Quite why these streets, in Dad's
metaphor, should have been in London and not, say, New York
(where bridge began) or Johannesburg (which was 'paved with

gold') was not clear to me at the time. I realise now that, although he learned to play in Scotland and spent most of his life in South Africa, the sort of bridge to which my father aspired, the bridge of elegant squeezes and dramatic coups, had its spiritual home in the smarter clubs of London. He could imagine the dashing men in tuxedos playing for high stakes while sipping vodka martinis and seducing women of impeccable breeding and pleasingly fluid morals.

In *Moonraker*, Ian Fleming reproduces one of the most famous hands in cards and uses it to rile the arch villain Sir Hugo Drax. The hand actually comes from whist, the precursor to bridge, and is known as The Duke of Cumberland hand. Towards the end of the eighteenth century, the Duke, the second son of George III, was a high-stakes gambler and was playing whist in a gaming house in Bath. The story goes that he was dealt the following hand:

♠ A K Q J
♥ A K Q J
♦ A K
♣ K J 9

Almost all the top cards! At the very least, he must make ten tricks in a no-trump contract and, if his partner has anything at all,

he must make twelve (a 'small slam') or thirteen (a 'grand slam').
But, without so much as a by-your-leave, the opponents bid seven
clubs. He doubles and they goad him into a rash bet, saying he
will not win a single trick. The Duke takes the bet, even though as
a gambling man he should have suspected something was up.
He duly makes no tricks, for these are the full hands:

NORTH

♠

♥

♦ Q 8 7 6 5 4 3 2

♣ A Q 10 8 4

WEST

♠ A K Q J

♥ A K Q J

♦ A K

♣ K J 9

EAST

♠ 6 5 4 3 2

♥ 10 9 8 7 2

♦ J 10 9

♣

SOUTH

♠ 10 9 8 7

♥ 6 5 4 3

♦

♣ 7 6 5 3 2

With clubs as trumps, the declarer (the person who first bid the suit in which the final contract is agreed) has only to finesse the clubs twice, trump two rounds of diamonds and claim the balance of the tricks.

It is said to have cost the Duke twenty thousand pounds.

In *Moonraker*, James Bond and Drax are playing for more modest, but nevertheless high stakes. They are at the Blades Club in London. They despise each other. As the game progresses, the stakes rise. Bond is deliberately offensive. He feigns drunkenness and insults his opponent. Honours are more or less even when Bond deals from a prepared hand. In bridge, as in so much else, Bond is prepared to break the rules in the service of his ego, his libido or Her Majesty's Government. M, his partner, has been warned that when the bidding gets a little wild he must keep quiet. The cards are dealt and Drax looks at his extraordinary hand. But Bond is the dealer and he opens with a bid of 7 ♣. Drax, sitting West, gulps a few times and wonders what to bid. He has no obvious slam of his own and, eventually, in impotent rage, he doubles for penalties. His partner leads a diamond and Bond's hand is secure. His trumps and suit length destroy the high card strength of the West hand. 7 ♣ bid and made and – more importantly – Sir Hugo Drax is fifteen thousand pounds in the hole. Round one to Mr Bond. No doubt they will meet again.

Fleming loved his bridge, and played regularly at the Portland Club and at Whites. The fictional 'Blades' is something of a mix of the two and an entirely appropriate setting for what Kingsley Amis described as 'probably the most gripping game of cards in the whole of literature'. With typical attention to detail, Fleming sets the scene, by evoking the animosity between Bond and Drax, but also through his vivid descriptions of the minor characters found in any rubber bridge club. There is General Bealey who 'doesn't know the reds from the blacks. Nearly always a few hundred down at the end of the week. Doesn't seem to care. Bad heart. No dependants. Stacks of money from jute.' Or Duff Sutherland who was 'an absolute killer. Makes a regular ten thousand a year out of the club. Nice chap. Wonderful card manners. Used to play chess for England.'

I suspect that Dad imagines himself 'making a regular ten thousand a year' (or its modern equivalent). He may well imagine himself playing chess for England. But, in fact, he does neither. What he does is teach his son that trumps have magical properties. 'Everyone gets dealt some cards,' he says. 'It's what you make of them that counts. Just remember to trust trumps more than you trust your high cards.'

For Dad, character will always count for more than wealth.

5. Latitudes

PARENTS APPEAR TO their children fully formed and it is many years before they question who they are and how they came to be that way. They are simply taken as they come. He smells of tobacco? OK. He listens to the radio with a faraway expression on his face? So be it. Silence becomes him? He wears long socks and has two-tone legs? His shoulders shake when he laughs? He stalks the house in dark rages that come and go without warning? He sometimes uses curious words that no one else uses and when you ask why he talks about some place called 'the auld country' or even 'home'?

The bit about home confused me a little but I did not dwell on it. By the age of seven, I had come to accept that words mean different things, especially to adults. Home for me was our house in

Wembley, Pietermaritzburg. It had a veranda at the front and a wild fig tree in the garden. There was a woodshed I thought of as Brazil and a carport for Antarctica. It didn't bother me at all that the world I mapped out in our garden bore only a passing resemblance to the globe in my bedroom. The top lawn was the Atlantic Ocean. The courtyard outside the kitchen was Siberia. Round the back of Antarctica, somewhere near Australia, were some rooms where Margaret lived. Margaret was the maid. She was big and black and called me 'Mafuta', which means fat. She meant this as a compliment.

At night, I lie on the sitting-room floor with the globe in front of me. My father calls out place names and I have to find them. Mostly he goes for exotica. Popacatepetl and Lake Baikal. Some are easy, like Salisbury, and some are hard, like Riga. Occasionally we reverse the game. I find places on the map and spell out their names. I have no memory of catching him out. He seems to know everything, even before I say it.

'Just using the available evidence,' he says. 'Just reading the signals.' He tamps his pipe and looks at me with a smile. 'Remind me to teach you one day.'

In bridge, players will use cards that have no other value to tell their partner something. This is called signalling. At its simplest it is a way of telling your partner whether you want him to continue playing a suit, or to switch to something else. Alan Truscott, in the *New York Times Bridge Book*, explains it like this: 'Signals come in many guises. When you are making your first discard, you can play a high card to say, "I have strength in this suit and want it led," or for a low card to say, "I am weak in this suit and do not want it led."'

Of course, it is not only your partner who reads the signals. Your opponents are watching too.

If you are going to signal, you should signal as 'loudly' as possible. If you have an honour sequence of, say, Q-J-10, then you will discard the Q. If you discard the J, it means you don't have the Q and so on. 'But,' according to Truscott, 'there are two things to beware of: Firstly, only signal when you think the message will help your partner. Very often a signal will help the opposition and should not be given. This requires judgement, and experience is the only guide... If in doubt, do not signal.'

Dad watches me tracing the contours of the globe with a finger. Before I can read the name on the map, he says it himself. He knows where my finger is before I do. He knows that I am likely to choose places with short names in preference to places with long names. He knows only big cities and big rivers make it on to the globe. He is reading the signals.

'Ask me more places,' I say to Dad.

'Jedburgh,' he says, but he has to spell it out because it is not pronounced as it is spelled. And his accent makes it worse. When he says Scottish place names, he exaggerates the pronunciation, which makes them even less intelligible. I scour South America for a place called Jedburgh.

'Try Scotland,' he says.

I find Scotland, but Jedburgh is too small to appear on the globe.

'It's not here,' I say crossly. 'There's no such place.'

Dad has a point to prove, so he goes over to the bookshelf to get the old atlas. There he finds a map of southern Scotland.

'That's Jedburgh,' he says. 'That's where your grandfather was born. Now find Istanbul.' I find Istanbul without too much trouble. In Dad's old atlas it is still called Constantinople.

'They say that's where bridge began,' he says. 'I think it was about the time I was born.'

Well, yes and no. Dad was born in the autumn of 1926 and the rules of the bridge we play today – contract bridge – were first formulated towards the end of 1925. But it came from a long tradition of whist. In 1742, Edmund Hoyle published a short book called *A Short Treatise on the Game of Whist, Containing the Laws of the Game, and Also Some Rules Whereby a Beginner May, With Due Attention to Them, Attain to the Playing It Well.* The original is now in the Bodleian Library in Oxford although many pirated copies exist and later editions are housed at the British Library in London. According to Alan Truscott, one of the great bridge writers, Hoyle's book was 'the biggest seller to make its appearance in the 18th century'. He was soon able to introduce similar guidance for other games and by the time he died in 1769 (at the ripe old age of ninety-seven) he was the accepted 'arbiter of law and order in all games'. It was Hoyle who set the standard for the most remarkable feature of the game. In a world occupied by cheats and gamesmen, cardsharps, thieves and brigands, he insisted upon a 'Code of Ethics and Fair Play' that appears, with very minor changes, in the laws by which we play contract bridge today. Hoyle would not have approved of Bond's use of prepared hands. Not even in the interests of Her Majesty's Government.

Little is known of the early history of bridge. In the Bodleian Library, there is a pamphlet by an anonymous author dated 1886 and entitled 'Biritch or Bridge Whist, or Russian Whist'. It describes the general features of a game that it claims is a variation of the Russian game of *Vint*. The writer, Mr Keiley, was a member of the Khedival Club in Cairo. He writes, 'bridge was the principal card game played there at my entry and had, so the members told me, long been so.' Some years later the *Daily Telegraph* carried an article by a Mr O.H. van Millingen who had lived in Constantinople in 1879 or 1880 and remembered 'a very interesting game called Biritch that became very popular in all clubs and dethroned the game of whist'. He included as evidence a letter from a friend called Graziani who had worked as a translator in the Italian embassy in Constantinople. Written in 1922, Graziani's letter said that nearly fifty years previously he first played bridge in the home of Mr Georges Corionio, manager of the Bank of Constantinople. Also present at the game was 'a Rumanian financier' by the name of Serghiadi, who taught the others the principles of the game. Some historians have speculated that the game was played by British troops while serving in the Crimea. As many as 14,000 soldiers would have been stationed in and around Constantinople.

And yet the game didn't arrive in the United Kingdom for some decades or, if it did, no record survives. Perhaps, as the American Contract Bridge League's *Official Encyclopaedia of Bridge* notes, 'its creators were killed at Balaklava or Inkerman'. The game is, of course, a variation of games that have been played for centuries under a variety of names. But Mr Keiley's letter appears to have been the first time the name 'bridge' was used in writing. It is not certain where the name came from. In 1854 or 1856, a resident of Istanbul, Metin Demirsar, wrote that, 'As part of a course on Ottoman history and architecture ... my guide mentioned that

British soldiers invented the game bridge while serving in the Crimean War. The card game ... got its name from the Galata Bridge, a bridge spanning the Golden Horn and linking the old and new parts of European Istanbul, where they apparently crossed every day to go to a coffeehouse to play cards.' Thierry Depaulis wrote a comprehensive *Histoire du Bridge* in which he concluded that the game had started in the diplomatic community in Constantinople, and he associates it with words from Serbo-Croat and Ukrainian. Rex Mackey, another historian of the game, notes these various attributions and particularly the suggestion that the name derives from the Russian word 'Biritch'. Sadly, there is no such word in Russian and he concludes that perhaps 'it was a Slavonic mode of address to a female partner'.

In 1894, Lord Brougham introduced the game of bridge to the Portland Club in London. He had, apparently, learned it from army officers in India and it differed from whist in one particular respect: the dealer (or, if he declined, his partner) had the prerogative to name the trump suit, after which the bidding ensued. In 1904 – and again the exact circumstances are not known – there was another innovation. It was agreed that the player willing to commit to making the most tricks would be able to name the trump suit. As Alan Truscott notes, 'it took some time to work out the details. It was easy to decide that a bid of two ranked higher than a bid of one. It was not so easy to settle the rank of the suits. Spades started at the bottom, but then became the top suit, with the result we know today: in ascending and alphabetical order, clubs, diamonds, hearts, spades, with no trump outranking them all.' In other words, a bid of two spades is higher than a bid of two hearts. The highest possible bid is seven no trump.

Over the next two decades, various innovations came and went. The scoring changed. In India, four officers of the Raj, including Hugh Clayton, later knighted as a member of the Indian Council of State, developed a system of scoring in which there were bonuses for making game (ten tricks), a demislam (eleven), a small slam (twelve) and a grand slam (all thirteen tricks). French players adopted the same principles and incorporated them into another version of whist called 'plafond'. Players were 'encouraged by the scoring table to climb to their plafond, or ceiling'. Auction bridge made no such demands. If a player bid one spade and made four, he scored his game just as if he had bid them and, according to Rex Mackey, this was 'naïve and pleasant for sweet old ladies and retired warriors at the nineteenth hole, who found it difficult to add up to four anyway. Accordingly, the apologetic attempts to introduce Plafond into England were met with the same sturdy resistance as their grandfathers had accorded the Reform Bill.'

But plafond did introduce the idea to a young American in Paris that tricks made only count if you bid them first. It was here in 1919 that Harold Sterling Vanderbilt, known to his friends as 'Mike', played the game at the Traveller's Club and mulled over it for some years before introducing it to the United States as contract bridge.

In our sitting room in Pietermaritzburg, Dad and I are spinning the globe.

'And you?' I ask. 'Where were you born?'

'I was born here,' he says, pointing to the coast of Fife. 'Kirkcaldy.' But Kirkcaldy does not feature on my globe either. We have to retreat to the atlas to find it on the northern shore of the Firth of Forth, almost directly across from Edinburgh. Even now I can hear the way he says it, with a soft Scottish burr and a faraway look. The 'l' is silent so that the 'caldy' of Kirkcaldy rhymes with 'body'. I try it, but it feels wrong. I pronounce both 'k's and the 'l'.

Dad laughs. 'Well, maybe we'll take you there one day,' he says.

It occurs to me now that Dad never said where his mother was from. Years later Cal and I visit one of his brothers who tells me that she came from Edinburgh from a mix of Scots Catholic and Irish Catholic stock. Granny Quinn was Irish, but Granny Lee was Scots. The Balfours were lowland Presbyterians until my grandfather met Rose Quinn and fell in love. He converted when they married.

At this point in my life, I have not met my paternal grandparents. They are names from faraway, like places on a map. And while I think of Dad as a 'father', it doesn't really occur to me that he is a 'son'. I recall vividly the moment my son made the connection. We were in London and I was on the phone to my mother in South Africa. I called her 'Mum'. Cal, who was a little over four at the time, looked at me sharply.

'Why did you say that,' he said. Why did you call her "Mum"?'

'Because she's my mother,' I said. 'I'm her son just like you're my son.'

'You never told me that,' he said.

'Oh.'

There was a silence while he thought about this.

'So you and me are both sons?'

I nodded. 'Every man is somebody's son. You can't be a man unless you're a son.' But, for Cal, the thought foundered on the realities of inner-city London life and he went on to list any number of his contemporaries who had no one that they could acknowledge as their father.

'They're still sons,' I said, 'even if they don't really know their father.'

'OK.'

That night I wrote down this conversation in a diary I keep for Cal. Strange what you reveal when you think you're writing about someone else.

6. Daft at cards

I REMEMBER SUMMER dew and winter frost and the way the bees used to hover over the fallen flowers from the jacaranda tree. David is allergic to bee-stings. Jackie and I are not. She and I catch bees and offer them to David like gifts. We are vastly amused when one stings him. My mother purses her lips and prepares a compress of bicarbonate of soda. Dad shakes his head with a smile and remembers his brother Robin, who could start a fight in an empty room. Dad had three brothers and he was the eldest. He knew them well when he was young and hardly at all when he was old. He knew his sister better. She moved from Scotland to live near us in Durban. I remember her smoky voice and her laughing eyes.

And I remember being driven into 'town' and being taken to Catechism. This takes place in the school across the road from

St Mary's Catholic Church in Pietermaritzburg. There we duti-
fully recite articles of the Profession of Faith. We learn about the
Liturgy and the Holy Sacraments. We read stories from the
Gospels and discuss their relevance to modern life. We are told to
love our neighbours and to honour our mothers and fathers. We
are told about the importance of prayer in Christian life. We learn
about transubstantiation.

'It's like magic,' David explains.

I follow him to the altar to take Holy Communion. The Body of
Christ sticks to the roof of my mouth. I wonder if I should
mention this at confession.

Afterwards, Dad takes us across the road to the museum where
there is a regular morning film show. Usually these are some kind
of science documentary. One morning, we watch a film about the
annual sardine migration that causes such excitement along the
coast of Natal. Vast shoals of fish swim inshore. People scoop
handfuls of them into buckets, nets and plastic bags. The narra-
tor tells us the fish are doing what nature intended. He says this
suicidal migration is 'part of the natural order'. As far as he is
concerned, things have always been this way, and they always will
be. In another film, scientists study animals by catching them in
nets. In some films they catch the animals by hand. A man will
run into a herd of impala and grab two or three by their hind legs.

One emerges holding five females. He has a wild look in his eyes and blood running down one cheek. In another film, Lake Kariba comes into being. They pour concrete and 'relocate' the wild animals. These films are full of a world in which it seems important to be big. Big men in short trousers with large moustaches talk about Africa in the same way my father talks about mowing the lawn. It's dirty work, but someone's got to do it. Trouble is, when Dad mows the lawn small pebbles are apt to get caught in the rotor blade. They shoot out to one side and shatter the windows in the sitting room.

'Don't go there,' Mum warns. 'Get some shoes on.'

We seldom wear shoes. Our days in Pietermaritzburg are spent with our feet bare and our noses burned by the sun.

In one film, yet another man with a moustache tells us that Africa is drifting apart. The Great Rift Valley is becoming wider. The whole continent is on the move. I make a mental note to ask Dad about this. I wonder which way Pietermaritzburg will go. I worry that our house will be split in two.

Dad says he thinks we are on solid ground. He is sure the crack in the ceiling is not caused by continental drift. We're sitting on the veranda at home, waiting for the stars. I like to see Venus rising and to watch Betelgeuse emerge small and bright and orange, like a parrot on the shoulder of Orion. While we wait, Dad is reading Robert Louis Stevenson's *Kidnapped* to me.

Like the *Requiem* and *A Child's Garden of Verses*, *Kidnapped* holds a special place in the Balfour family's affections. My brother has the same name as the book's hero, David Balfour. I have the same name as David Balfour's father. Stevenson took the surname from his mother, Margaret Balfour, to whom we are distantly related. His full name was Robert Lewis Balfour Stevenson, but he dropped the 'Balfour' when he started writing and adopted – an author's affectation I imagine – the French spelling of 'Louis'. When Dad reads *Kidnapped*, it is not just because it's a cracking yarn. It is a rite of passage into a mythical world.

In the book, the wicked uncle Ebenezer sells his nephew David Balfour into slavery. We only learn at the end of the book that Ebenezer came to own the estate when he and his brother fell in love with the same woman. A deal was done; Alexander followed his heart and Ebenezer backed off on condition he got the estate. The story begins when David, the son of Alexander, the elder brother, comes to 'claim what's his'. His ship is wrecked off the west coast of Scotland and he escapes. He teams up with Alan Breck, a wanted Jacobite rebel and together they make their way across Scotland to Edinburgh.

Stevenson liked to write 'in the vernacular' and Dad likes to read it that way. For me, the story is easy enough to understand, but the words are hard to follow. And so progress is slow. We have to recap at regular intervals. Dad loves these strange Scottish words. 'Birstle,' he says, and 'Clanjamfry'. 'Whillywhas' is another favourite. He unpicks each word gently, giving each syllable its full weight. He plays with them, like a man spooning honey from a jar. He turns the spoon smoothly to stop the honey from falling.

'Ye muckle ass!' he quotes when I spill juice on his knee.

When I ask him to explain different words, he is a little impatient. 'Words like that mean what you want them to mean,' he says. But then he explains anyway. Birstle means to get sunburned. Clanjamfry is another word for rabble. He reserves a special reverence for whillywhas, which means flattery. He loves the word and hates the idea. Dad is not given to overstatement, although he has mastered the raised eyebrow of approval. He can make me feel special with one direct glance because he so seldom meets our eyes.

In storytelling, his approach is like that of Stevenson. Writing to his friend, Charles Baxter, about the book, Stevenson says, 'it is more honest to confess at once how little I am touched by the desire of [sic] accuracy. This is no furniture for the scholar's library, but a book for the winter evening schoolroom when the tasks are over and the hour for bed draws near ...' Stevenson has 'no more desperate purpose' than to 'steal some young gentleman's attention from his Ovid, carry him awhile into the Highlands and the last century, and pack him to bed with some engaging images to mingle with his dreams'.

It's a challenge Dad loves and he warms to his task. He is seated on a chair with his feet up on the low wall that surrounds the veranda. Beyond the caps of his shoes, I can see the orange lights of Pietermaritzburg begin to twinkle in the gathering dusk. The green trees of my world become sombre shadows in the night. Dad has a lovely resonant voice. After retirement, he will read books on to tape for visually impaired people to enjoy. In his hands – or rather on his tongue – Stevenson's strange Scottish words take on a life of their own. The 'Heugh of Corrynakeigh' becomes a place of mystery and wonder. He plays with the words, like a juggler.

He can keep three or four 'Rs' in the air at a time like Miriam Makeba singing 'The Click Song'. He rolls them around in his mouth and swaps them from side to side. He sends them floating on to the night air like a clown blowing ping-pong balls. I am sitting on his lap as he reads to me. His body rumbles with the reverberations of his deep voice. Sometimes he reminds me of a fire-eater I once saw in a photograph in a magazine. The man had big sideburns and a shaven head. He wore only a kilt and big boots. He looked like a human volcano. Dark purple and red tattoos flowed down his torso like lava. In the photograph, the spectators recoiled from the ball of fire that shot from this man's mouth. One mother covered her child's eyes. Another had her hand to her chest as though crossing herself. But when Dad speaks aloud there is nothing to fear, even though somewhere deep inside powerful forces are at work. With my head resting on his chest, I can hear what goes on in the middle of the volcano. Sometimes he reads sentences again, just for the sound of them. When the heroes fight, I can hear – no, *feel* – the guttural whoosh as Dad expels the air from his lungs. 'Oh man,' he cries on Alan Breck's behalf. 'Am I no' a bonny fighter?' He shoots a bright-orange flame of Highland profanity out into the evening air.

I imagine the sparks dying on the azaleas.

As darkness falls, the twins, Castor and Pollux, appear above the edge of the plane tree. Beyond the jacaranda, I can see the Southern Cross. From the kitchen, we hear my mother calling us in for supper.

'Come on,' says Dad.

Reluctantly, I follow him indoors. It is only recently that my sister and I have been allowed to eat our suppers at 'big table'. We used to eat them in the kitchen with Margaret for company.

Dad sits at the head of the table and prepares to carve. The vegetables are in front of my mother who sits to his right. My mother does the cooking, but it is my father's taste that dictates the diet. It comes straight from his childhood. Nothing fancy. Nothing spicy. Just good, wholesome 'meat and two veg' as long as one of the 'veg' is potatoes. When, occasionally, Mum makes a mild curry he breaks instantly into a sweat. Beads of perspiration form on his brow. They race each other down the canyons of his frown. In later years, my mother tries to vary things a little. It doesn't work with Dad. All he wants is his meat and two veg. He's not much interested in anything else, except perhaps beer and a dram.

We always sit in the same places. In bridge parlance, we would say Dad is 'sitting South', which is not really anything to do with the points of a compass. North, East, South and West are just names of convenience to describe the relations between the players. In bridge, both the bidding and the play of the cards go clockwise. The dealer deals and he opens the bidding. The person on his left bids next. The bidding carries on until three players in succession have passed. Whoever first bids the suit in which the final contract is agreed is known as 'declarer'. It will be his task to play the hand. The person to his left plays the first card, which is known as 'leading'. Once the first card is led, declarer's partner puts his cards on the table. They are face up, for everyone to see.

At that moment all the players know where twenty-seven cards are – thirteen in their own hand, thirteen in dummy, and whatever card has been led. The challenge is to work out who holds which of the remaining twenty-five cards.

At our dining-room table Dad is sitting South, then Mum is sitting East. Jackie and I sit West, opposite Mum. And North, down the far end of the table, is David. If he played bridge, he would be Dad's partner. But he doesn't.

It is an arrangement that will last the next decade.

Dad is playing the hand in the sense that he directs whatever becomes the topic for discussion. 'Let's bat that one around,' he likes to say when we ask him a question. And our hearts sink, for we know there is no escaping it. Everything is up for debate, even though he knows all the answers in advance. This evening, he has not finished with his bridge lessons. In fact, they're only beginning.

'First thing is, what's in your hand,' he says. 'What's it worth?'

We wait.

'Not only the obvious things,' he says as he carves. He puts two slices of pot roast on a plate and passes it to Mum. It is going anti-clockwise, the opposite way to bridge. Mum ladles on the vegetables and passes the plate to David. He calculates whether the next plate will have more or less and, in the hope of better luck, he passes it on to my sister, Jackie. Jackie is polite. She passes it to me. I have no one to pass it to.

Mum pushes the gravy boat across the table, while Dad rehearses the basics.

The aim of the game is for each partnership to try to take as many tricks as possible. Actually Dad is not convinced about this. While winning as many tricks as possible may be the aim of the game, it does not necessarily follow that it is the aim of the people playing the game. For if it was, they would surely behave differently. In his series of books on *Bridge in the Menagerie*, Victor Mollo put it like this. 'There is too much stress everywhere on the art of winning and not nearly enough anywhere on the art of losing. Yet it is surely the more important of the two, for not only do the losers pay the winners but they clearly enjoy doing it. Were it otherwise, they would have stopped playing – or taken up winning – long ago.

'Success at bridge, in fact, depends less on winning than on extracting the last ounce of pleasure from losing.'

Success and failure – Kipling's twin impostors – are old friends to Dad, and he treats them both the same. He thinks, in essence, that you get what you deserve. His favourite bridge book – voted recently by the membership of the American Contract Bridge

League as the best bridge book of all time – is S.J. Simon's *Why You Lose at Bridge*. 'Skid' Simon was one of the creators of the Acol system of bidding and a mainstay of the English game before, during and after the Second World War. An immigrant from the wilder reaches of the Soviet empire (he hailed from Dniepropetrovsk), Simon arrived in London without any visible means of support, graduated from the London School of Economics and earned a crust writing for publications as diverse as *Punch* and *The Economist*. It was not long, however, before he 'found his true metier which was writing, living, expounding and, to an extent, creating contract bridge'. The thesis of *Why You Lose at Bridge* is that you lose because of *who* you are. 'It is true that I do not know the particular individuals in your Bridge Club. But I know them well enough for your purpose. For all Bridge Clubs, from the Portland to the tenth-of-a-cent Suburban, are only repro-ductions of each other in varying degrees of wealth, with the identical assortment of inhabitants. The accents may vary but, from the Bridge point of view, representatives of the various breeds are found in all of them.' Victor Mollo characterised them as animals. Simon gives them a human face. His characters are called Futile Willy, Mr Smug, the Unlucky Expert and Mrs Guggenheim. Futile Willy knows too much and understands too little. In trying to do the 'right thing' he invariably gets it wrong.

Mr Smug plays good bad bridge and usually wins. Mrs Guggenheim is a hopeless case, a deer caught in the headlights every time a card is led. She often partners the Unlucky Expert, who loses because he insists on trying for the best possible contract rather than the 'best contract possible'. The former is determined by what cards people have. The latter depends on who is playing. For them, as for those in Mollo's *Menagerie*, character is fate and, while they can learn to mitigate against the worst defects, they cannot eliminate them. For, as another leading bridge player told me recently, 'Whatever defects of character you have will be worse at the bridge table. Every chink in your character will be exposed and magnified. Sadly the same is not true of your strengths, although they may, against all odds, still be evident.'

But Dad glosses over this.

'First question,' he begins, 'is, what's your hand worth? What have you got there? Diamonds or fool's gold?' In South Africa, the idea of fool's gold is very powerful. In our top-heavy, centralised economy more than 50 per cent of the country's foreign earnings come from gold.

There's a system for assessing the value of a bridge hand. It was devised by Milton C. Work, the foremost writer on auction bridge in the days before contract bridge existed. Work assigned

a value to each of the high cards. This is how the American
Contract Bridge League now describes it:

> *Hand Valuation*
>
> The ace = 4; the king = 3; the queen = 2; the jack = 1.
> In addition to giving points for high cards, points are
> given for the shape of the hand. A five-card suit = 1;
> a six-card suit = 2; a seven-card suit = 3; and an eight-
> card suit = 4. Once you have valued your hand, the
> next step is to bid according to its strength and shape.

For a time, the Work 'count' was replaced by a system devised
by a man called Ely Culbertson. Culbertson is known as 'the man
who made contract bridge' and we shall hear much more about
him later. But when in the 1940s Charles Goren took over from
Ely Culbertson as the doyen of American bridge writers and
teachers, the Work count was restored to its proper place as the
best method for assessing the relative strength of a hand. On his
count, there are forty 'points' available in a pack of cards, made up
of four aces (sixteen points), four kings (twelve), four queens
(eight) and four jacks (four). An average hand therefore has ten
points. A hand with more than ten points is an above-average
hand; one with fewer is not.

The following advice therefore applies:

> With 0 to 12 points, pass.
>
> With 13 or more points, open the bidding with one of your longest suits.
>
> With 15 to 17 high-card points and a balanced hand (one where all suits are represented with at least two or more cards), open 1NT (no trump).

Except, of course, if you play a different system. And, in any case, many strong players will open 'light', which is to say with a hand with less than thirteen points and also give much greater emphasis to 'length' (that is, the number of cards one holds in a particular suit, hence the valuations given to the count, above) and less to high-card strength. It is not uncommon, for example, to see a player with eleven points and six diamonds open with a bid of 1 ♦. Bidding is not only a conversation with your partner. It is also a battle with your enemies, and the point of bidding is to talk to your partner and to prevent your opponents from talking to each other. You have to calculate the penalties too. In duplicate bridge, you get thirty points for each trick bid and made in spades and hearts, and twenty points for tricks bid and made in clubs or diamonds. For no trumps, you get forty for the first trick and thirty thereafter. One hundred points gives you 'game' and game is worth 500 points if you're vulnerable and 300 if you're not. The target bids, therefore, are 'three' in no trump, 'four' in a major suit or – if you really have to – five in a minor suit.

From the beginning, Dad's bidding is aggressive. He likes to upset the opponents. And he likes to play the hand, even if it means he fails to make his contract. There's a saying that 'one down is good bridge'. In my father's world, two down sounds like fun and three down is positively imaginative. I learn to regard all his opening bids as highly dubious and to listen carefully to his second bid to see whether or not it bears any resemblance to what I might consider to be a rational progression from his first bid and my response.

And it's not just about point count. 'Shape' is also important. Do you have a long suit? Do you have a void? In a trump contract, a void gives you as much 'control' as an ace because you can trump anything led in that suit. And – crucially – do you have a fit? Does what you have complement or weaken what your partner has?

'Because once you have a fit, you're in business,' Dad says. 'Once you have a fit you can tell your partner what you want to do.'

The Role of the Responder

The partners on a bridge team have certain roles to
play. The opening bidder describes his hand to his
partner. The partner becomes the captain and assumes
the role of deciding on the best denomination and the
best level for the final contract. The partner of the opening
bidder knows more about the combined strength of the
two hands after hearing the opening bid and looking at
his own hand.

This is a nice idea, but I have yet to meet the opening bidder
who thinks he has entirely relinquished the captaincy to his
partner. Certainly not Dad. For him, the opening bid was merely
a demand that his partner tell him something about his hand so
that he would then know what to bid next. But with this information he agreed entirely with Skid Simon, who often said that
the key was to 'Bid What You Think You Can Make'. Do it quickly
and cleanly. The moment you know what you want to play in, bid
it – and in the process keep your opponents quiet. 'The fewer your
bids, the fewer chances you give your opponents to get together...
Keep your bidding simple. Approach when you must and take
the direct route whenever you can.'

'I think you're going too fast,' says Mum.

'Am I?' Dad pauses in mid-flight to see the vacant expressions of his children. David has eaten all his food and is waiting to ask for more. Jackie is almost done. Dad looks a little crestfallen.

'Och, well,' he says, 'another time.' He busies himself with seconds. In this, he is unfailingly polite. He offers each of us in turn before he takes the biggest helping for himself.

In *Kidnapped* David Balfour and Alan Breck have their falling out over a game of cards. They have taken refuge with Cluny MacPherson, a Jacobite leader in hiding. Cluny is a good host, but often drunk. 'We were no sooner done eating than Cluny brought out an old, thumbed, greasy pack of cards, such as you may find in a mean inn; and his eyes brightened in his face as he proposed that we should fall to playing,' Dad reads.

But David Balfour has not forgotten the lessons of his childhood. He could have pleaded fatigue, but instead he chooses to lecture the old man on the rights and wrongs of gambling. 'Now this was one of the things I had been brought up to eschew like disgrace; it being held by my father neither the part of a Christian nor yet of a gentleman to set his own livelihood and fish for that of others, on the cast of painted pasteboard,' David Balfour tells them. Dad is smiling as he reads it. David retreats to his bed where he tries to sleep off a fever. But Breck and Cluny set to playing.

It is – as Stevenson well knew – a familiar tale of woe. At first, Breck wins, but soon he is gambling away the little money he and David have saved from the shipwreck. David wakes from his fevered sleep and suspects the worst, which Breck confirms.

> 'David,' says he at last, 'I've lost it; there's the naked truth.'
>
> 'My money too?' said I.
>
> 'Your money too,' says Alan, with a groan. 'Ye shouldnae have given it me. I'm daft when I get to the cartes.'

Dad is many things, but daft at cards isn't one of them.

7. Capsizing an Optimist

THE 'GOLDEN AGE of apartheid' – in that terrible and ambiguous phrase – coincides with my family's moment of greatest cohesion. We three children attend our local school, to which we walk, footloose and fancy-free. Our weeks are full of sunshine and friends. Each evening we eat our meals round the dinner table at which Dad invites us to 'bat that one around'. 'That one' seldom includes South Africa's politics. In these matters my mother is liberal (with a small 'l') and Dad is conservative with a marginally larger 'c'. In any case, it is not something they like to discuss. Where could such discussions lead? It is better to say nothing. With my globe I indulge in imaginary travel. I climb the Andes and float across the Serengeti in a balloon. I read *Swallows and Amazons* and *The Hardy Boys*. Pietermaritzburg seems like a little island in the ocean of my imagination. It has no connection to the rest of South Africa. My reference points are a world that comes to me from books. The books are published in New York and London. Very few of them come from Johannesburg or Cape Town.

It is also the time of the grand gesture. Dad likes to make them just as he makes speculative leaps at the bridge table. There was the trip to Europe. There is the *Optimist*. On a whim, Dad decides to build a small dinghy on which we will learn to sail. He clears a space at the back of the house and orders a 'build it yourself' kit from the manufacturers. And one Friday evening he settles in to build the boat. David helps, while I watch. The size of the challenge just about matches the powers of his concentration and later it occurs to me that for him this is part of the appeal of bridge. A hand of bridge takes perhaps six minutes to play. Some may take a little longer, others may be quicker. In simple hands, the declarer may 'claim' his tricks after the first few tricks have been played. It is a curiously satisfying experience. The bidding has been fierce. You've arrived in a contract, which may or may not 'make'. You set off hesitantly, not sure which is the best line of play to follow. But the tricky questions resolve themselves easily. West's singleton king (known in bridge parlance as 'stiff'; a singleton three is merely single, but singleton king or queen is always 'stiff') falls to your ace. The finesse you take on trick three works. The contract is secure and you can spread your hand with a flourish and claim. Of course, you need to be pretty confident you are right before you do this. If you claim and the opponents do not accept your claim, they can force you to play out the rest of the hand with your cards exposed.

Dad is confident he is right.

Tournament bridge can be a gruelling affair. National or World Championships may take a week or two and by the end of them the winners have played as many as several hundred hands of bridge. It is exhausting. Dad played tournament bridge before I was born, but really he had no patience for it. But for the length of each hand his concentration is complete.

To watch him pick up a hand is like seeing a hawk in the sky. He hovers above the play, taking it all in. Nothing escapes his attention. He knows that each hand is a story and that the action is only now about to begin. It starts with the first bid; it ends only with the last card. And so he floats on the thermals, watching the layout. He knows what he has; there are only thirty-nine more cards to discover. The first bid will show some of them. He owns the table. He can wait.

At the bridge table, for example, Dad is happy to make any number of safety plays. A safety play is one where declarer maximises the chances of making a contract by forgoing the possible opportunity to make one or more overtricks. A common safety play involves giving up an early trump trick in order to be sure of retaining control of the trump suit later in the hand. It means, for a moment, that declarer no longer has the lead, but it is done secure in the knowledge that the lead will return.

Bridge requires both fire and patience. In some of the great partnerships, the qualities are supplied in different measure by each partner. Rixi Markus, one of the greatest players ever to grace a bridge table, had a highly tempestuous relationship with Fritzi Gordon, a fellow Viennese who later came to England. The two were 'fire and ice'. Victor Mollo wrote of them that, 'Few men played as well as Fritzi Gordon. No woman plays better. But it is with men, rather than with the women, that she should be compared for Fritzi's bridge is intensely masculine and he-man stuff at that. Where Rixi Markus is fiery, Fritzi Gordon is icy cold.' It was a partnership that worked. It was not necessary for them to be the same, as long as they worked together. In playing together Markus learned a truth with which most bridge players will agree in reflective moments, but which many are prone to forget in the heat of the moment: 'I have learned by bitter experience that, unless you treat your partner as a good friend, you will not achieve results. It does not matter how little or how much he knows about the game: it is up to you to make him feel safe and confident in order to get his best game from him. Allow him to take part in the bidding and the play, and do not treat him with disdain or indifference even if he is far below your own standard.'

The same sort of dynamic appears to have been true of one of the other great British partnerships. Terence Reese and Boris Schapiro first played together in 1944 and continued to do so for many years. 'They hit it off immediately,' John Clay writes in his *Tales from the Bridge Table*. 'At the card table, Reese was more like an academician, studious and diligent, reminding people of the classical scholar he had been. He was always strong on logical analysis. His single-minded concentration at the table was famous and all his energies were bent to the task in hand.' Boris Schapiro was born in Lithuania in 1909. He came to Britain after the Russian revolution and first played bridge at the Doncaster Conservative Club while he was an engineering student in Sheffield. 'The central core of his personality is aggressive self-confidence,' Guy Ramsey wrote of him. 'The compact body is held with a certain arrogance of posture; the regular features are embellished with a small, almost foppish moustache...' Like Markus and Gordon, these two were 'fire and ice'. Where Reese was calm, Schapiro was ebullient; where Reese was rational, Schapiro was impulsive. John Clay concludes of him that he was 'an instinctive player, able to do the right thing at the right time without needing to know why. But they played together for many years, with extraordinary success, notwithstanding the accusations of cheating that were to blight their later years.'

Zia Mahmood, one of the few superstars of the modern game, has a more inclusive approach to partnerships. He has played over the years with almost every player of international standing, but he acknowledges Michael Rosenberg, a New York-based options trader, to be his favourite. Together they have won many honours. Nevertheless, Mahmood appears to like playing with a variety of people. It enables him to avoid falling into routines. Every hand becomes even more of an adventure. In *Bridge My Way*, he writes, 'rather than worry about individual bidding-system preferences, I preferred to know the individual characteristics of my partner. Was he cautious or aggressive? Was he a good declarer or a good defender? Modern or old-fashioned? Just knowing these things would be a huge advantage. But it was a lot to find out in one minute.'

Or a lifetime. Mahmood and Rosenberg know each other's game intimately. And yet sometimes even they misunderstand each other. At the United States team trials in the spring of 2005, for example, they played together as part of the Welland team. Rosenberg, sitting West, held a very strong hand:

♠ A K Q

♥ A K Q J 7 4 3

♦ Q 4

♣ 7

The opponents opened the bidding with 1 ♦ . The question is
what does Rosenberg bid next? He has ten certain tricks with
hearts as trumps. Equally, unless his partner has a couple of aces,
he has three certain losers. The right contract is 4 ♥ . But how to
get there? And how to be sure not to miss out on a slam? If his
partner has an ace or a void, there might well be a slam available.
At the other table the bidding went 1 ♣ , Double, Redouble
(showing four or more diamonds), pass, 1 ♦ . At which point West
bid 4 ♥ and everybody passed. The contract is unbeatable – but
nor are there any other tricks available and 4 ♥ is the best contract
on the hand. It gives a plus score (East-West were vulnerable) of
620 points.

But Rosenberg and Mahmood are always looking for more.
Never settle for ten tricks when thirteen might be possible. And
so after South opened 1 ♦ , Rosenberg bid 4 ♦ . By their system
this showed a very strong hand in an (unspecified) major and
invited Mahmood to show any strength he had with a view to
exploring slam. But Mahmood had no strength to show and no

suit to bid. I was watching the play on the Internet at the time and even over the distance of several thousand miles I could sense the tension in the room. What do you do when your partner has made a bid you don't fully comprehend? And when you have nothing? The situation was further complicated because the opponents were playing a Precision Club system which meant they might have opened 1 ♦ with as few as 2 diamonds. Mahmood thought a long time before deciding to pass. He must have calculated that his partner's bid was natural. Of course the opponents passed too. And instead of making 10 easy tricks with hearts as trumps, Rosenberg found himself going down five in diamonds, a shocking result on the cards.

But it happens. I like to think Rosenberg would do the same again.

Over the course of a single weekend the *Optimist* takes shape. It's an ugly little boat with a snub nose and a flat hull, but Dad is very proud of it and so are we. It is, according to the brochure, 'quite simply, the dinghy in which the young people of the world learn to sail'. Dad builds like he does everything else. He assumes he knows how it's done. Only when that fails does he read the instructions. Undeleted expletives hang in the air. I remember the smell of sawdust and varnish.

Mum covers polystyrene floats in bright canvas. We launch the dinghy with all due ceremony on a sunny day at Midmar Dam. The dam is a little way out of town. There are grass slopes to sit on and wattle trees for shade. The *Optimist* is too small for Dad to sail, but David takes charge. I am a little in awe of David's ability to handle the boat. He finds my willingness to do what he tells me useful. When we play together there is no need to negotiate who takes control of the hand. He is my big brother. After a few weekends of 'pottering about' he takes me out into the middle. There is only the faintest wind. All over the lake, other dinghies wallow disconsolately on the glassy surface of the water.

'Come on,' he says. 'Let's see if we can sink it.'

This strikes me as a very silly idea.

'OK,' I say.

'You climb the mast,' he says. 'And lean out as far as you can.'

Like I said, it is a silly idea. I climb the mast, lean over, slip and fall in the water. David thinks this is hilarious.

Some time later we arrive back on shore.

'How was it?' Dad asks. He's fishing for compliments.

'I fell in,' I say.

'We tried to sink it,' David says. 'But we couldn't.'

''Course you couldn't,' says Dad. 'I made it.'

'Mum made the floats,' says David.

8. Welcome to our world

ZIA MAHMOOD COMPARES learning to play bridge with falling in love. On the cover of his bridge memoirs, *Bridge My Way*, he writes, 'If you've never been in love – don't read this book.' His book is for crazy people, for people who believe in 'fantasy, romance and obsession'. His book 'is for all those people who ever started doing something and became so involved in it that they lost track of time, because the thing I started doing was playing bridge and the time that went so painlessly by was my life'.

I learned bridge from my parents and later I came to love it. But it took me a long time to work out what I had learned and why I loved it. Dad may have been right – everyone likes bridge; they just don't know it yet – but he glossed over the difficulty that some people never get to know it. Even Ely Culbertson, the man who made the game a worldwide phenomenon, initially struggled to like it. And it seems he never really fell in love with the game, even though he was a man always on the verge of love. For him, it was a business proposition. An entertaining one, to be sure, but first and foremost it was business. Culbertson first came across the game – it was still auction bridge then – on a boat trip from Europe to New York in the autumn of 1913. Strolling on deck, he saw four people playing cards. Naturally, he was drawn to them. He was already very good at several other games, including poker and *Vint*, which he had learned while in prison in Chechnya. The game he saw on board the ship, he says, 'resembled the Russian Vint except that the dummy was exposed and the bidding was very limited. Every now and then I heard one of them exclaim, "Partner, may I play?" "Pray do!" "No spades, partner?" and the father, who was a cautious businessman, sometimes added, 'What, no spades? Please look among your clubs."'

Culbertson stopped to watch them play. Writing in his memoirs, a curious book called *The Strange Lives of One Man*, he recalled, 'The game was called *bridge*. I was urged to join, but after a few sessions I gave up in disgust. *It's a stupid game*, I thought.' The italics are Culbertson's own, and I suspect that a great dollop of hindsight's wisdom informs this version of events. The more likely story is not that he thought it a stupid game, but that he did not wish to appear to be anything other than the best player, and for that he needed more than three minutes to study it.

A year later, he is reintroduced to the game by 'a girl' whose parents are 'rich enough to send her to one of those foreign schools where, in a mere two years, a perfectly nice girl is usually turned into a finished product of useless knowledge and imitation glamour'. Part of which, even then, was a working (though possibly useless) knowledge of bridge. He is dissatisfied with the arbitrary nature of the rules. 'Who made them?' he wants to know. What were they thinking of? Why didn't they do it like this? What is the underlying philosophy of the game?

I read into his recollections a different question: why would I be interested in a game if I am not the one running it? Perhaps there is gold in those hills. His father was an oil prospector. Culbertson was looking for a dark seam of money to call his own. He continued to play, but he irritated his partners and opponents alike with his brooding. He never ceased his infernal questions, especially the one that troubled him most: 'What is there about this silly game that they understand and I don't?' When the others merely laughed at him he resolved to become 'the best player on the planet'.

There is a similar story of the experience of Charles Goren, the man who took over from Culbertson as 'the face of bridge'. Like many others – notably Culbertson and later Zia Mahmood – Charles Goren first got into bridge because of a young woman, who laughed at his 'gaucherie and lack of skill' when she hosted a bridge party in Montreal in 1923. Goren was a law student at the time and recalled that the young woman's laugh 'was like putting a knife through me'. He went home to Philadelphia, bought Milton Work's *Auction Bridge* and set about making good his resolve that he would not 'sit down at a card table until [he] knew how to play the game'. He quickly became an exceptionally good player and attracted the attention of Milton Work, who also came from Philadelphia, but it was not until 1936 that Goren stopped practising law and turned his attention full-time to the world of bridge.

If you learn as a child, as I did, it cannot really be love at first sight. I was too young and bridge is too complicated and too difficult. You can't love it until you know it – and it takes time to get to know. But it was *something*. Mahmood, however, was hooked from the beginning. 'I was trying to get better acquainted,' he writes in *Bridge My Way*, 'with an attractive young woman whom I knew only slightly. The good news was that she finally agreed to meet me. The bad news was that the venue was a bridge party ... I had, of course, told my date that I could play.' Unsurprisingly, the bridge element of the party was a disaster and Mahmood performed 'embarrassingly badly' although he 'managed to save [himself] from complete exposure'. But he did fall in love that evening, and not with the young woman. Bridge was the object of his desires. 'I became enthralled; the spark had been lit and soon became a fire. No, not a fire, more like a furnace.' Mahmood started to read everything he could get his hands on and soon found himself swept away by the world of bridge, its life and its characters. He read about Ely Culbertson who was 'to bridge what Muhammad Ali was to boxing', and about the Italian 'Blue Team', the *Squaddra Azzura* that so completely dominated the world of bridge in the 1960s until they were challenged by Ira Corn and his Texas Aces.

There is little doubt that, by the time Mahmood came to the game, bridge was 'a world' and that this world is not just about the four people around the table. I have before me, for example, a copy of a British Armed Forces recruiting poster from 1916, which the then War Office used to invite men to come and fight in the trenches. The poster, printed in full colour, was widely distributed in England and Ireland at the time and shows three men in the trenches settling in for a game of bridge. The men are clearly 'chaps': one has a pipe, another is happily brandishing the ace of hearts, and all three have sculpted jaws and perfect white teeth. They surround a suspiciously clean, linen-covered crate serving as a card table. Only the sandbags behind them and the butt of a rifle leaning against the white cloth suggest that life in the trenches is any different from, say, the officers' mess at Sandhurst or an evening at the club in Curzon Street.

'Will you make a fourth?' runs the caption on the poster and the implication that trench warfare is one long game of cards is clear. So, too, is the implication that bridge is synonymous with all that is good, with all that 'we' were fighting for. The poster is not without its ironies. It was distributed in Ireland as well as in Britain in 1916 and photographs exist, for example, of it on the walls of Dublin's Four Courts shortly after the city (and, indeed, the courts) had been shelled by the British forces.

My father is unlikely to have known the image. It was from 'before his time', but he would have understood the sentiment. I once heard him call the bridge table his 'small square yard of freedom', and he meant it literally and metaphorically, and probably metaphysically as well.

The question 'Will you make a fourth?' is older than that, of course, and has been asked for as long as the precursors of bridge – whist and plafond and other games – existed. C.S. Forester's Hornblower novels are set in the early nineteenth century and in, for example, Lieutenant Hornblower we find the eponymous hero saying, 'I am always glad to make a fourth,' before explaining to his companion that a good many men from the services 'drop in [to his club] for a game of whist'. The same scene occurs, almost exactly, for example, in Balzac's *Scenes from a Courtesan's Life*, first published in the 1830s. Charles Dickens poses the question in a private letter written in 1841. For him, as for others, the question was metaphorical as well as literal. To make a fourth was to enter a purer world and to leave behind you the noisy and dislocated distractions of other worlds.

This is the 'world' of bridge. Writing in 1925, Milton Work predicted that 'The Auction Bridge World is entering upon a new era – the era of stability. During the formative period, deficiencies have been supplied, undesirable features eliminated, and every innovation has received the test of experiment and experience.' He was wrong. Unfortunately for Work and his many and varied sources of income from auction bridge, the books and magazines, teachings and columns, radio lectures and personal appearances and all the other cacophonies through which a sporting celebrity may derive wealth and fame, the era of stability on which he was so confidently embarking was about to end. Auction bridge was about to die and be replaced by contract bridge, the game we know today. The middle of the third decade of the twentieth century was a difficult time to be making predictions, for only three years after he wrote these words Work lost a considerable part of the fortune he had derived from bridge in the stock market crash of 1929. He later found it necessary to take up again the lucrative bridge activities from which he had at that point retired.

And yet I find Milton Work's confidence a little seductive, precisely because of his use of the word 'world'. Others use it too, for example, *The Official Encyclopaedia of Bridge*, a work of such monumental and exhaustive proportions that I struggle to lift it with one hand and which runs, in the edition I have beside me, to some 1,000 pages. Here again, we find the phrase, this time on the cover, on which we are told that the 'world of bridge has undergone a revolution since the fifth edition of this book was published in 1994'. Not only a world, then, but also one in which revolutions occur, heads of state are chosen, deposed, assassinated – if only in character – and replaced. A world in which the language of politics is scattered liberally through its literature. As Zia Mahmood puts it, 'Squeezes are always "inexorable", entries are always "carefully preserved", a 4–1 trump break is always "bad news". Anything above a ten is never discarded but "spectacularly jettisoned". Gory images are all-pervading – one doesn't just double, one "wields the axe" and an 1,100 penalty is invariably a "massacre" or a "bloodbath".' Similarly, we find that attacks develop, weapons are neutralised, slams are forced and defences are planned. It would take little effort, Mahmood concludes, to turn the average bridge column into a Tarantino script.

This is the bridge world. I like it. It is a comfortable place to be. But David doesn't like it and he doesn't play in it. Not if he can help it. I am not sure why, but I have another picture which offers a cautionary tale. It is a facsimile of the illustration by Marcus Stone for a scene from *Great Expectations* in which Pip is playing a rubber of whist at the house of Miss Havisham. At first glance, we may admire the players' focus on their game. The men are hunched thoughtfully over the table. They are playing in these pairs: Pip and Miss Havisham; Mr Jaggers and Estella, the object of Pip's affections. Both Estella and Miss Havisham are concentrating hard. But as we look more closely at the faces of the older woman (for the men's backs are turned to us) we see the dark eyes, the scowling face, the clenched fists. She has a desperate and hungry look, a feral focus on survival. And we realise that she has more about her of the heroin addict than of a gentleperson of leisure. She is trapped in a world – that word again – from which there is no easy escape and in which, as Pip nonchalantly tells us, all her hopes come temporarily to nothing.

Of course, for Pip, as for Dickens, the game speaks volumes about so much else. 'Of the manner and extent to which he took our trumps into custody, and came out with mean little cards at the ends of hands, before which the glory of our Kings and

Queens was utterly abased, I say nothing...' For it is not about the cards at all. 'What I suffered from, was the incompatibility between his cold presence and my feelings towards Estella,' and the cards (especially the 'mean little ones') are only the outward expression of a far deeper turmoil. In this case, the fourth member at the table is Mr Jaggers whose cold indifference drives Pip to distraction. The text does not say who took all the money in the end but one takes it from Miss Havisham's expression in the illustration that she lost, and that she held Pip accountable for the fact and the scale of her losses. It was Sartre who remarked of football that it is 'endlessly complicated by the presence of the opposing team'. Bridge has the additional complication of one's partner.

Or, in my case, my family. Somewhere, round about the time I turn ten, my family becomes complicated.

9. Falling in, falling out

It starts when my father changes jobs. For a time, he commutes between Pietermaritzburg and Durban, but in the middle of 1972 we move to the old house on the hill, overlooking the distant Indian Ocean. It is here that Dad will spend the last thirty years of his life.

The change of job has not been easy; his career path – this should have been the moment of transition from engineer to senior management – is interrupted at precisely the moment the children are most expensive. There are school fees and clothes, sports equipment and holidays. We eat vast amounts, particularly David and I. He has grown tall and wiry. I have merely grown. Perhaps from the pressures of work or perhaps because he is tired, Dad starts to drink too much. By 1976, it is serious. We see it in different ways, but say nothing. I notice it when Dad can't catch a rugby ball. We're playing in the garden on a Saturday evening. David is in his school team. He sends long 'torpedo' passes the length of the lawn. I am learning to run on to the ball, to 'take it at speed'. Dad tries the same. The ball knocks into his knees. He stumbles and falls. When he gets up his knuckles are grazed and there is blood running down one knee.

'Tough game, rugby,' he says, but none of us is fooled. Nor do we know what to do. We share his embarrassment. For weeks afterwards, he will pick at the scab. David and I continue to throw the ball to each other. Wherever possible, we play around Dad, rather than with him. I've seen him do it at the bridge table. I've seen him do it with me. Occasionally, we are cruel about it. We set up dummy runs at Dad and run circles around him. David has a wicked sidestep and he uses it to good effect. We joke in Afrikaans about his 'sidestep'. It's a pun on 'stumble'.

We start to call him 'the old man'.

At the dinner table, there are shouting matches. We are seated in our usual places, which puts David in the line of fire, as it were, directly opposite Dad. The food gets passed around in the normal way. Dad carves, Mum does the vegetables. But our discussions are no longer free-ranging. We no longer take up Dad's offer to 'bat that one around a little' because there is no telling where the conversation will go. Quite often, it goes nowhere, but at other times it ends in furious arguments without purpose or resolution.

One night, my parents have a furious row; I can't remember why. Dad storms from the room, shouting, 'That's a lie.' I go to bed early and lie awake listening for the tense aftershocks from the earthquake. I have been there for some time when Dad comes through to my room. He knows the argument is 'his fault' and he has come to apologise.

'I'm sorry,' he says. 'But don't worry. Everything will work out fine.'

For the first time in my life, I don't believe him. How can everything be fine when your family are crying?

The fights seem to coincide with supper, when Mum most wants the family to be together and Dad is most angry at the world and his failures at work. He takes his anger out on the family.

Jackie and I keep our heads down, but David is too tall.

After supper, we play bridge. It becomes a form of peacemaking. At the bridge table, Dad is not angry at himself or the world. He does not shout. Here he continues to shine. He can play bridge even when he is drunk. His body doesn't work properly, but his mind does. He struggles to shuffle and deal, but he reads the cards easily and fluidly. It is as though he has entered 'the zone' that top athletes describe. He is in the 'pure serene' of Chapman's

Homer, while we sit, 'silent on a peak in Darien'. Wide-eyed and in awe, we shuffle and deal.

Dad wonders whether anyone will notice if he has another beer. At some point, he has started to brew his own ales, to 'put his chemical engineering skills to some use'. The beer he makes is heavy and yeasty and quite unlike the lager brewed by South African Breweries. Our house has some 'outbuildings', which is where the maid lives but also where Dad has his workshop and a 'studio'. Here he starts to experiment with brewing. Vats arrive and bottles. There are brewpots, fermenters and airlocks, bottling buckets and hosepipes. There is a machine for putting the tops on bottles and another for washing them. There are the ingredients too, sacks of hops and malt, yeasts of one sort and another and a big drum of sugar. And there are things to measure with. To get the beer 'just right', you have to test the temperature and measure the alkalinity. You have to watch your enzymes and beware of excessive diacetyl. It's not easy brewing beer, Dad tells us. There's a science to it. You have to get everything just right at every stage of the process, from cleaning the bottle – 'Here, scrub those out for me, will you?' – to making sure you put the cap on just right.

'We don't want any air getting in,' says Dad. 'No, no, no. We don't want that at all.'

What we want is for this to stop, but it doesn't. From time to time, it has mildly comic effects. In brewing, the more 'fermentables' – sugar, corn syrup and so on – you put in, the higher the alcohol content. Dad overdoes the 'fermentables'. From time to time, bottles explode, leaving beer on the walls and glass on the floor. The studio is at the bottom end of the garden, near the road. Sometimes it gets burgled. The thieves find only beer. They drink some and steal the rest. The next day, the police find them comatose by the side of the road, a bottle of Dad's beer in one hand.

'Try some,' says Dad, but I decline.

Beyond our door, South Africa is at war. In 1975, 'we' invade Angola and begin our increasingly brutal war of destabilisation against the newly independent countries of Mozambique and (later) Zimbabwe. On 16 June 1976, policemen fire on schoolchildren demonstrating in Soweto. Crowds take to the street and more violence follows. Many children are killed. Dad declines to get involved. He condemns the 'anarchy' of the protesters, but he cannot quite bring himself to approve of 'the Boers'. He has always refused to learn or speak Afrikaans and he indulges in the ridiculous snobbery of English-speaking white South Africans that allows them to 'look down' on Afrikaners.

The question of conscription arises. In 1978, I receive my first call-up papers to the South African Defence Force. I announce that I will not go. I have not yet decided whether (forgive the pretension) 'I will go to prison or into exile.' Like all fathers, Dad has to have a view – but I don't know what it was. He never says anything one way or the other. Perhaps he thinks I am old enough to make up my own mind. Perhaps he doesn't care. For me, neither of these is completely satisfactory. Angrily, I rehearse the arguments to myself. He should have a view? He has been a soldier? He fought against fascism?

But Dad says nothing. The questions are put to one side and instead cards appear on the table. When we play bridge, a kind of calm descends on the room, but David is not there to witness it. We laugh every time a finesse fails. We remember to draw trumps, lest we end up 'walking the streets of London'. We signal loudly and clearly. In the studio, a beer bottle explodes.

We go one down, which is good bridge.

We let the game smooth over a multitude of emotions. In the fifties, Samuel Barber wrote his comic operetta, *A Hand of Bridge*, the libretto for which describes with uncanny precision the world that is social bridge at any time between, say, 1925 and the present. The piece starts with the formalities of the game, each voice bidding in turn. Nobody is vulnerable but, as the characters begin to speak their inner thoughts, things take on an altogether more sinister tone.

David, a 'florid businessman', is playing with his wife Geraldine, who (as the libretto helpfully puts it) is 'middle aged'. Their opponents are Bill, a lawyer, and his wife Sally.

Sally is an airhead. The bidding progresses and she soon finds herself playing dummy – again. 'Once again, I'm dummy. Forever dummy,' she moans, to Bill's alarm. He reads more into the lament than is actually there. Dummy, he thinks, what does she mean by dummy? Is she talking about me? Does she know? Have I been found out? For his thoughts turn immediately to his lover, Cymbaline.

'Cymbaline, Cymbaline, where are you tonight?' he asks. 'On whose mouth are you murmuring senseless night words with your geranium-scented breath?'

Their opponents have other concerns. Geraldine wonders what has got into Bill. He is playing distractedly, and mistakenly trumps one of his own winners. What is he thinking of? And why does his foot no longer seek out hers under the table?

There's an easy answer to that, but Geraldine does not dwell on it. Instead, she contemplates the desperate barren years ahead, unloved and with no one to love. All the men in her life – her father in his photograph, her 'stock market husband', her 'football son' – are more or less useless in this regard. All that's left is her ailing mother who 'could have loved me had I let her'. But the years have not been kind in this regard. Too busy with her own affairs, Geraldine has neglected her mother and now 'there she lies in her pain, cocooned in her illness, an indifferent stranger, hatching for herself the black wings of death'.

This is heady stuff indeed, and I feel a certain sympathy for Geraldine. It is not easy to be past the first flush of youth, with one's shoulders and legs thickening a little, and one's husband's (and lover's) attention straying. But on the surface the game progresses and the players call out the cards as they play them. Bill is in control of the hand, though not, quite, his emotions. He continues to play, wondering all the while on whose mouth Cymbaline might at that very moment be breathing her geranium-scented breath. It should be him. It should be me! But his troubles are as nothing compared with the silently repressed David, the more or less useless stockbroker whose particular dream is not only to be his own boss but also to be rich! To be powerful! To be a man! As he plays, his desires grow ever more fantastic. He longs for the money and the fame, but he doesn't stop there. He also wishes for an 'alabaster palace in Palm Beach'. He wants it filled with 'twenty naked girls, twenty naked boys' all of whom will have no other purpose but to spend their days 'tending to my pleasures'.

But he knows it will never be. His epitaph will read, 'Worked for

Mr Pritchett every day, and every night played bridge with Sally and Bill.'

And so the hand and the piece reach their climax. The contract – they're playing in a contract of 5 ♥ – appears to be made. The cards are shuffled for the next deal. Silence fills the room.

In bridge, little is said, though everything is felt. I wonder what Dad was thinking all through those years.

It gets worse as the decade passes. I miss the brunt of it because I am away at boarding school. Before we moved house, my brother was sent to a Catholic boarding school thirty miles away. He came home only at weekends. But then we moved to the house on the hill. David became a day scholar and I was sent away to a different boarding school, an Anglican school. Around this time we stop going to Mass. Dad is beginning his

> ... melancholy, long, withdrawing roar,
> Retreating, to the breath
> Of the night-wind ...

The 'sea of faith', Matthew Arnold says in *Dover Beach*, was once 'at the full'. But no more. The Second Vatican Council was the beginning of the end for Dad. This was the Catholic Church's attempt to address a changing world. Called by Pope John XIII, the Council brought many changes to the Church, not the least of which was the introduction of 'the vernacular' to parts of the Mass. It sowed the seeds of doubt for Dad, and over the years they took root and grew. I remember once how I came home from school and told Dad about something that happened during Mass. Although mine was an Anglican school, they made special provision for Catholics. There were about ten of us, and on Sundays we would go down to the 'crypt' beneath the school chapel where a Catholic priest was waiting to perform the Mass. One year, I acted as altar boy. But disaster struck. The priest's hands were shaking – I didn't think it was just communion wine on his breath either – and, after the blessing, after transubstantiation, he spilled some wine on the altar cloth. The horror! After Mass, the priest asked me to fetch a bucket of water. He washed the altar cloth in it and then insisted I help to drink the water. All of it. It would not do, apparently, to leave the blood of Christ lying around.

I had been moving away from my childish faith for some time, but this is where I date my own departure from the Catholic Church. Dad seems to be keeping time with me. I tell him the story. 'Och, well,' he says, 'it's all bullshit, really.' He does not go to Mass any more, and he does not take us. I suspect he thinks confession would take too long. I think also he is just plain embarrassed. It is too much to look the priest in the eye. At this time, Dad is not looking many people in the eye. He blames himself, but he acts like it's their fault.

In 1978, David leaves home. We four that remain – when I am not at boarding school – eke out the decade in silence. Sometimes, we play bridge. More often, we bury ourselves in books. It is a dismal time for everyone.

In 1980, I leave home to go to university in Cape Town. Every year I receive a new set of call-up papers to the SADF. One Christmas, a school friend comes home from Angola in a body bag. The country is under the control of P.W. Botha, who is playing politics with his tri-cameral parliaments and renaming of this or that instrument of the apartheid administration. But really he is a military man. His 'solution' is repression in every form. I have long since decided that I will leave the country in preference to 'going to the army' or 'going to prison'. The only question is when. While at university, it is possible to defer military service. After I graduate, I can defer it for another year by taking a teaching job in a government school. But, by the end of 1983, I can put it off no longer. It is time to go. My girlfriend and I head for Zimbabwe and from there to London. Mum, Jackie and David drive from Durban to Harare to see me off. Dad stays at home.

I don't remember saying goodbye.

10. A house of cards

TWENTY YEARS LATER, on the evening after Dad's funeral, I walk through the old house. The guests have all gone and darkness comes quickly. A couple of lamps are lit; outside, the garden is bathed in black ink and the neighbourhood dogs are barking. Across the valley, the lights go on one by one. It is the night of the new moon and a light cloud covers the stars. The air is warm. In the garden, the silhouette of the flat crown is swallowed by the black sky. There is no wind; the azalea bushes are still. I slip outside. I close the door carefully, so as not to wake my mother.

The garden has shrunk over the years. When my parents bought this house on the hill, it came in three parts. There was the house and the surrounding lawns, together with the swimming pool and the tree, which even then covered the entire lawn in its shaded embrace. On the western side of the house, there was the driveway, some vegetable gardens, some old outbuildings and, below a right of way through to the neighbour's property, another patch of land noted mostly for its thriving avocado trees. This patch of land was known as 'the triangle' for its shape. To the east, where the house looked out towards the distant Indian Ocean, the land fell away sharply into the valley. Beyond the crest of the hill, invisible from the sitting room, lay a wild and untended hinterland known as 'the paddock', which I assumed was because the previous occupants had kept horses. Three tall blue gum trees, some hundred yards distant, mark its bottom edge. The treetops are just visible from the sitting-room window.

But now the garden is smaller. Over the years pieces have been sold off or knocked down. The triangle 'went' first, followed by the paddock, and then the tennis court on which somebody else's house now stands. The sales of the paddock and the court meant that driveways had to be built to either side of the house, so that the garden is shorter and narrower. The outbuildings too have been knocked down and replaced with yet another stretch of lawn. My father used this space to indulge his mild pyromania as he put a match to the piles of cuttings that seemed always to gather in this fertile and rich hilltop. It is hard to think of him now without also seeing the flickering flames, and the curls of sweet-scented smoke.

I return to the house and Jackie and I start looking through the mahogany chest of drawers in the alcove off the sitting room. It is here that the family memories are stored. There is one drawer for 'photographs (new)' and another for 'photographs (old)'. There is one for school reports, another for old letters and forgotten diaries. There are insurance policies and car registration forms, passports and old ticket stubs, all the paraphernalia of life, the documents that tell us who we are and where we have been.

And there is an entire drawer for packs of cards that somehow have never been thrown away, but have sat for years, for all my life and even longer. There are rubber bridge-scoring pads too, the stubs of pencils and a few scraps of paper with memorable hands scribbled in my father's illegible writing.

It comes as a shock now, perhaps thirty years after I first played with them, to see some of the cards and their designs, a shock of recognition, for it is more than twenty-five years since I lived at home, and possibly that long since last I opened this particular drawer. There are the Bicycle cards, of course, the staple product of our games and the world game, made by the American Playing Card Company and deeply ingrained in the psyche of any card player. But there are also ornamental cards and novelty cards, cards in ornate packs designed as bridge gifts, cards with photographs of places visited and places never seen, cards new and old, clean and dirty, cards with Greek gods and forgotten movie stars.

'This book could in theory begin with the invention of playing cards, probably in China a millennium ago,' says Alan Truscott in his 'anecdotal history of the game of bridge'. 'The evidence is scanty, and it may have been in India, or even further west. There is a pleasant legend that they were invented by the Emperor S'eun-Ho to keep his concubines amused in the year 1120, but he was, it seems, at least 140 years too late to claim the honour.' Others suggest that the invention worked the other way round – that it was the concubines of the imperial Chinese harem who invented cards. Another tale suggests that the earliest cards came from India where the wife of a Maharajah was irritated by her husband's habit of pulling at his beard. It is claimed she invented cards to alleviate her boredom – and to give her husband something to do with his hands. It seems more likely that cards were invented in China, where paper was invented. Even today, some of the packs used in China have suits of coins and strings of coins – which *mah jong* players know as circles and bamboos.

It is generally assumed that cards entered Europe from the Islamic empire (some blame Marco Polo), where records of the first card manufacturers come from Nuremberg in Germany in the fourteenth century. German card makers produced a variety of suits, some based on hierarchical representations of medieval society, and others using acorns, leaves, hearts and bells. At some point, these were replaced by representations of courtly human beings: kings and their attendants, knights (on horseback) and foot-servants. To this day, packs of Italian playing cards do not have queens, nor do packs in Spain, Germany and Switzerland. There is evidence that Islamic cards also entered Spain, but it now seems likely that the modern cards, which we call Spanish, originated in France, ousting the early Arab-influenced designs.

Cards came to the United Kingdom later than to the rest of Europe. The earliest mention dates from 1463 when manufacturers of playing cards petitioned Edward IV for protection against foreign imports. John Clay, in his collection of *Tales from the Bridge Table*, tells us, 'Kings Henry VII and Henry VIII played cards and the costumes on today's British and American court cards are those of this period.' In 1495, Henry VII issued an edict forbidding his servants and apprentices from playing cards except during the Christmas holidays (and amongst his private accounts at the time are several entries ascribed to 'losses at cards'). Elizabeth I took it further. She granted a monopoly in making cards (and protection from imports) to Ralph Bowles, and then charged him three shillings per gross for the privilege. By the early eighteenth century, cards had become popular, although the games played varied by class: 'The game of ombre was favoured by ladies, while the gentlemen preferred piquet. Clergymen and country squires played whist, and the labouring classes played all fours, cribbage etc.'

And the cards were taxed. The ace of spades became the card that was stamped to show duty had been paid; in 1765, it became known as 'the duty card', and the Stamp Office would keep a stock of pre-stamped aces of spades. Manufacturers were required to print the packs without a spade ace. 'When the tax for the pack was paid, the Office issued the ace of spades to complete the pack, and the deck could then be sold. The tax was abolished in 1960, when duty was back to three pence per pack. Yet today, most packs still display the ornate ace of spades for the manufacturer's design.'

I pick through the miscellany of our card drawer, remembering some, discovering others. Some packs are unopened. Others are worn from use almost to destruction. Recently, I was given one of the pack of cards used in a recent world championship. Nowadays, tournament cards have a regimental purity about them. They are strictly symmetrical about both axes. The colours are slightly differentiated – the diamonds are a different red from the hearts, and the spades and clubs are shades of grey and black. They have bar codes to enable the dealing machines to duplicate the hands. Every pack looks exactly the same. There is no story. But these cards in the drawer of our home in South Africa are different. I learned to play bridge with them.

11. People not cards

I REALISE NOW that bridge became a form of expression for Dad, a kind of storytelling where the story is on 'a loop' and repeats itself ad infinitum. As we learn to play, it becomes a favoured metaphor of his. It's how he talks about people. It's how he tells us about himself.

In his version of this story – in his version of *any* story – he is declarer. He made the contract and he will play the hand. He is the focus of attention, the centre of his small universe and far more important than his left-hand and right-hand opponents or 'East and West'. In our family, my mother and sister are East and West. In this scheme of things, declarer always sits South and declarer's partner therefore is North. Declarer's partner, the one who 'makes the fourth', is known as dummy. In French they call it *le Mort*, the dead, which is unkind both to dummy and to the dead. The fifth role belongs to the kibitzers, those who merely watch.

'Kibitzer' comes to us via Yiddish and German, from *Kiebitz*, the name of a type of plover with a folk reputation as a meddler, sticking its beak in where it doesn't belong. Expert kibitzers know that there are few pleasures in bridge greater than critiquing the efforts of those at play without having a financial or emotional interest in the outcome of the game. There are rules, written and unwritten, that govern the behaviour of kibitzers. Law II of the 'Laws of Duplicate Contract Bridge', for example, requires that a spectator should not look at the hand of more than one player, except by permission; shall not display any reaction to the bidding or while a deal is in progress; and shall always and everywhere refrain from conversation with a player during play. A stony and possibly reverential silence is required for the whole of the play. Once the hand is over, the kibitzer may, should he wish, guffaw loudly and make disparaging remarks about the parentage of the players, but he should bear in mind that the players have the right – in tournament play anyway – to have any kibitzer ejected from the room. And – which is most frustrating – kibitzers 'shall not call attention to or comment on any irregularity unless asked to do so by the tournament director'.

This is just as well. In my experience, kibitzers in their omniscience have an oppressive regard for the 'best possible contract'. In *Why You Lose at Bridge*, S.J. Simon makes the distinction between the 'best possible result' and the 'best result possible'. The latter, he argues, is more desirable because it takes into account not only your cards but also the people at the table. 'The professional is not concerned with playing good bridge. He is playing practical bridge. He is not interested in the best theoretical result on the hand – all he cares about is what he can score in the actual circumstances. It is no use to him that a small slam can be made on a squeeze if his partner, who has to play the hand, can't execute a squeeze.' Both he and Ely Culbertson famously argued that they 'play people not cards'. Easley Blackwood, who invented the game's most widely known bidding convention in the game, called his bridge book *Bridge Humanics: How to Play People as Well as the Cards*. There is much more to take into account than how the cards lie.

Kibitzers are too concerned with the 'best possible result'. There is something slightly unforgiving about them. Victor Mollo put it neatly. Who would wish to be, he asked, the sort of person who brings 'to the bridge table that gift for lightning analysis which enables him to tell at once why a patient had departed and how his life could have been saved'?

David is not much of a kibitzer. He prefers to do things than to watch. I am more of a watcher, but I am frustrated that, as my elder brother, he knows more than me. At the bridge table, this is no longer true. I know more than him. I like this.

Then there is dummy, which was my role as often as not when I played with Dad. It was where I viewed him from, tugging at his dark, bushy eyebrows, muttering to himself, humming a snatch of some work, Beethoven perhaps, and planning a coup of such devilish complexity that he would, in all likelihood, fool himself as well as his opponents. My being dummy was nothing personal; it was only that he loved to declare. He was a natural 'hog' and believed implicitly that 'it was in my interest as well as his to let him play the hand.'

'Hogs', those who want to play the hand no matter what the cost, are a well-known phenomenon in bridge clubs. The most famous 'hog' of them all is an invention of Victor Mollo who wrote several books starring 'the Hideous Hog'. 'H.H.' as he is known is one of several characters that populate the Griffins Club in central London. Over the years, Mollo came to realise that all the club players had their equivalents in the animal world, and the club, in his writings, becomes a menagerie in which the various animals behave true to their natures and to their cards. Mollo's series of books on *Bridge in the Menagerie* (later co-written with others) remain some of the best books on bridge. Of all of the characters it is 'H.H.' who demands the limelight, both for his brilliance and his insufferable arrogance. Dad would without doubt have agreed with Mollo that 'The word 'hog' ... should be an honoured title, not a term of opprobrium. On grounds of expediency it is obvious that the better player should be in charge, for the strong have a moral obligation to look after the weak, and who can be weaker than a weak partner, who can be more deserving of protection not only from others, but above all from himself?'

In fact, Mollo goes on neatly to subvert the Hog's view. 'The fallacy of the Hog's approach,' he writes, 'lay in assuming that the interests of partners are one and indivisible, that what is good for North is equally good for South and vice versa. That is at best a half-truth. Neither North nor South wants to lose, but winning may be all-important to South and of comparatively little importance to North. Leaving all moral considerations aside (and where else is one to put them?) it is indisputably in everyone's interest to play as many hands as possible.'

Ranged against declarer are the opponents, who may or may not include one's partner, whom Zia Mahmood has, with some justification, described as 'centre-hand opponent'. In Mahmood's world, 'centre-hand opponent' is the kind of partner who will make a doomed sacrifice bid of 5 ♣ instead of leaving one's vulnerable opponents in a redoubled contract of 4 ♠ in which they are certain to go at least three down (i.e. make only seven tricks instead of the ten they have agreed in the contract). In one particular hand that Mahmood describes, he does give credit where credit is due. 'My partner played the hand well, contriving an endplay against East which allowed him to escape for eight down...' The joke in bridge is that a partner is someone who sticks with you through the trouble you wouldn't be in without him. Bridge is full of anecdotes like the one about George Kaufman, who, in between writing Broadway successes, made himself into a top-class bridge player, and who one afternoon found himself playing with a woman of limited ability who duly proceeded to massacre a cast-iron contract. 'Madame,' he is reported to have enquired, 'when did you take up this game? Oh, I know it was today, but what time today?'

But you have to have a partner and it is as well to know with whom you are playing. S.J. Simon puts it like this: 'You must learn to play your players. And your partners more than your opponents. You must learn their strengths, weaknesses, predilections and obstinacies – and allow for them.' Zia Mahmood told me once in conversation of another great club player: 'This guy, frankly, he's an embarrassment. I mean, you wouldn't ever want him to come to your house. You know, he's not the sort of person you want to introduce to your mother. His clothes, his smell, I mean. But...'

But you would want him on your side. But you would rather be with him than against him. But, despite his looks and his disastrous personal hygiene, despite his debts, his alcoholism and his chain-smoking, despite his philandering and lies, despite *everything*, you know that in the end you can trust him because he plays good bridge and must therefore somehow represent all that is good and wholesome, progressive, honest and orderly.

And he wants to win, even more than you do.

As long as I was prepared to be dummy, I could escape being labelled a centre-hand opponent. In this sense, my relationship with my father was always sympathetic, and from a very early age I understood that the essence of playing with him was to share his brilliance, especially when it failed. It was better if it succeeded, of course, but there was no dishonour in losing. Icarus may have fallen from the sky, but he did it with style. Not for Dad the ignominious 'white legs disappearing into the green / Water' of W.H. Auden's *Musée des Beaux Arts*. To see Icarus as merely a 'boy falling out of the sky' was simply to have come to the story at the wrong moment. To have caught him in the ascendancy, with the wax still holding, was to see it in another way entirely. At that moment, anything is possible, just as a hopeless contract is possible up until, though not including, the moment the unfortunate 8–1 trump split is revealed.

'And even then…' Dad would have said, and one would have been expected to share with him the hopeless optimism that believes in the miracles of which he alone (or so he thought) was capable. In bridge, one's opponents have no interest in sharing anything. They are not impressed with your flair and precision. They lump all these attributes under the heading of 'arrogance' or 'idiocy' or possibly both, and either way they accord you only contempt or loathing, the latter being a form of grudging respect. They are there to frustrate you or, even better, to be humiliated and frustrated by you.

Officially, dummy's role is to sit silently while your partner makes an unholy mess of things or – more rarely – inadvertently rescues you from a truly awful contract. Like kibitzers, dummy is, by the Laws of Contract Bridge, forbidden from any number of activities. These laws are enforced with increasing severity the higher one goes up the bridge ladder. At home, the rules may be bent this way and that, but, in tournament play, this will not happen. But dummy is not forbidden everything. He may, for example, draw attention to irregularities in the play (which kibitzers may not) once all fifty-two cards have been played, though not before. In some countries, notably the United States, he may prevent a revoke (when a player does not follow suit, despite having available cards of the suit that was led) by asking his partner whether he has any cards of that suit. Laws 42 and 43 go into dummy's rights in some detail. He forfeits these rights if at any stage of the play he looks at his partner's or opponents' cards. But these are the laws as they apply to tournament play and sometimes to high-stakes rubber bridge. In more social forms of the game, we have a greater licence.

The name 'dummy' comes from an earlier version of whist, in which there were only three players and the fourth hand was open on the table for all to see, there being a kind of imaginary and silent player. In contract bridge, however, despite the rules and the nomenclature, the best dummies are highly active. They make the tea, refill glasses, summon more canapés from a passing waiter (signing the bill while they're at it) and bring updates on the progress of the cricket or the 3.15 from Turffontein. They live each twist and turn of the play. And they remember the play best, if only for the purpose of later berating their partner. They may not have the analytical skills or knowledge of the kibitzer, nor may they remember who held what cards precisely, or in what order they were played, but they have the correct emotional register with which to celebrate success or apportion blame. And sometimes dummy can help the play, with a helpful nudge here or a neat piece of misdirection there. On the rare occasions when he allows his partner to play a hand, for example, the Hideous Hog is an animated and dangerous dummy. 'A remarkable facet of the Hog's self-confessed genius was his ability to control the play as dummy,' says Mollo. The Hog does this through a combination of dishonesty and gloating, usually at his partner's expense but undoubtedly also in his interest. And the interests of better bridge, of course. He distracts the opponents, lays false trails, talks loudly over the play, eats and drinks anything within range, scratches himself noisily and is merciless in his dissection of his opponents' many faults when his partner has, through some gross gaffe, made the contract.

Such an elaborate metaphor. I wonder where it all began.

PART III

WHEN HIS WORLD WAS YOUNG

12. An evening in Panama

CONTRACT BRIDGE – the history of which is little known prior to 1925 – began on 1 November of that year. In his history of the game, *The Walk of the Oysters*, Rex Mackey called it 'the time of the great hangover' in Europe. Nothing seemed certain. 'Despite the affable gentlemen who signed the Locarno Treaties "forever preserving their nations from the scourge of war," everywhere there was unemployment, crises and gloom, gloom, gloom.' Britain was under the leadership of Stanley Baldwin, now in his second stint as Prime Minister, having previously been deposed by the attentions of David Lloyd George. Unlike our current leaders for whom it is necessary always to appear busy and for whom to relax is to risk vilification, Baldwin was content to while away long afternoons at 10 Downing Street playing auction bridge with ladies of reportedly dubious morals.

In the United States, however, the mood was more optimistic. Coolidge presided over his exuberant nation with the disinterest of the wealthy patriarch, his mind on other deals, while – despite the 18th Amendment – his people sported themselves in the clubs, theatres and arenas of the country's thrusting new cities. Again, Mackey puts it neatly. 'While the Rum Fleet lay offshore, New York became a vast speakeasy and the civic affairs of Chicago were guided by the competent hands of Alphonse Capone; in the deep South the Dayton Monkey Trial put the Bible in the ring against the *Origin of the Species*; and on a November night in his stateroom on the S.S. *Finland*, Harold Sterling Vanderbilt shuffled a deck of cards.' F. Scott Fitzgerald also published *The Great Gatsby* in 1925, John Logie Baird demonstrated that television was more than just a dream, and in South Africa a modest Dutch dialect, having acquired an army, became the language of Afrikaans.

But, for the time being, the United States appeared to be a nation at play, and Vanderbilt was one of its greatest players. A yachtsman of international stature, a natural athlete and one of the finest card players of his generation, his was a roving and inquisitive mind, always willing to experiment and explore. So it was that, while on that cruise ship and passing through the Panama Canal in the fall of 1925, he shuffled the pack of cards and looked around at the three men who accompanied him.

'Gentleman,' he said to his assembled companions, 'let me show you a new game. It may interest you.'

Indeed. It interested them and generations to come with a passion bordering on the ridiculous. Even so level-headed an individual as the late Lord Lever could remark, 'Chess is challenging but bridge is the stuff of life.' Rex Mackey put it like this: 'Housewives, who hitherto thought dummy was a baby's pacifier, banded themselves together to the permanent ruin of their husband's digestions. It interested newspaper and publishers, films and radio, big business and ballyhoo merchants. It added a new dimension to leisure, and it also provoked murder, mayhem and domestic strife ...'

The newly leisured classes, temporarily free from the scourge of war, needed something to do in the evenings. Something that didn't cost money and didn't require them to 'go out'. Something which you could do whether you were eight or eighty. Something which allowed for conversation, but which filled the silences. Something accessible yet challenging.

Something that everyone would like, whether or not they knew it yet.

Vanderbilt, for whom bridge was only one of many things to occupy his mind, recalled how he came to devise the rules: 'Many years of experience playing games of the Whist family were,' he wrote, 'a necessary prelude to acquiring the background and knowledge needed to evolve the game of Contract Bridge... I compiled in the autumn of 1925 a scoring table for my new game. I called it Contract Bridge and incorporated in it, not only the best features of Auction and Plafond, but also a number of new and exciting features; premiums for slams bid and made, vulnerability, and the decimal system of scoring which by increasing both trick and game values and all premiums and penalties was destined to add enormously to the popularity of Contract Bridge.'

Many have written that Vanderbilt invented 'contract bridge' but this appears not to have been the case. The name had already been used in other contexts – W. Somerset Maugham, a fanatical player, mentioned a game called 'contract' in *Ashenden*, his semi-fictional account of spying for Britain (amongst which exploits he numbers attempting, but failing, to prevent the successful uprisings in what was then known as St Petersburg) – and others had suggested variations on auction bridge at various times over the preceding decade. Maugham first refers to bridge in *Smith*, the 'first play in the history of theatre to open with a game of bridge'. That was in 1909. At other times, he took the view that 'bridge is the most entertaining and intelligent card game the art of man has so far devised'. In his short story *Christmas Holiday*, he wrote these lovely, if hyperbolic, lines:

'It only made the difference of a trick.'
  'A trick? A trick? A trick can make all the difference in the world.'

And that was just auction bridge. In contract bridge, more is at stake as one only scores points for tricks both bid and made. The committee presiding over the publication of the 1917 Rules of Auction Bridge, largely written by Milton Work, had considered and rejected the principle of making the contract rather than the auction the centrepiece of the game. Vanderbilt's achievement was that he created a package that could be sold, whole, to the public. As a figure of note, his endorsement was a very attractive part of the package.

He goes on: 'An ideal opportunity to try out my new game presented itself while I was voyaging shortly after completing my scoring table with three Auction Bridge playing friends on board the steamship *Finland* from Los Angeles to Havana via the Panama Canal, a nine-day trip. At first, we were at a loss for a term, other than 'game in', to describe the status of being subject to higher penalties because of having won a game. Fortunately for us, a young lady on board the *Finland* solved that problem by suggesting the word vulnerable.'

History does not record the lady's name, although we do know the names of the other three players, through the efforts of Alan Truscott of the *New York Times*. On the fortieth anniversary of this voyage, he contacted the U.S. Lines shipping company and got hold of their passenger lists. Vanderbilt in his records referred to them only by their initials, but Truscott was able to identify them as Frederic Allen, Dudley Pickman and Francis Bacon. The *Finland* reached Balboa on 31 October 1925, too late to proceed through the Panama Canal or for passengers to go ashore. Francis Bacon III, in 1975, the sole surviving member of Vanderbilt's foursome, recalled that on that night the lady who suggested 'vulnerability' as an added dimension to the game was allowed to join their game of plafond and attempted to suggest some exotic and impractical changes based on a game she said she had played in China. This so irritated Vanderbilt that, the next day, while the *Finland* passed through the Canal, he worked out the scoring table for contract bridge which remained virtually unchanged half a century later, except for the points awarded to no-trump tricks (bid and made) then earning thirty-five points each. Today, the first no-trump trick is worth forty points and subsequent ones thirty, meaning that 3 no trump makes 100 points, which is to say 'game'. On that night, 1 November, the game became contract bridge, scored under Vanderbilt's new rules.

Vanderbilt ensured it immediately had enough weight behind it to last. He created the first bidding convention. It is one of the peculiar charms of the bidding in bridge that it so accurately reflects real life: 'everything is about something else'. Bids can and do have a multiplicity of meanings which can only be understood if one knows under which convention the bid is made. Since clubs are the lowest ranked of the suits, the lowest bid one can make is 1 ♣. Vanderbilt created a convention (he called it the 'Club Convention', although everyone else called it the 'Vanderbilt Convention') that required a bidder with a strong hand of any description to bid 1 ♣. Subsequent bidding would reveal the true nature of his strength. Vanderbilt also wrote the first major work on contract bridge. And he inaugurated the Vanderbilt Knockout Team Championship. He won it twice and endowed it with sufficient cash that today winners still receive a silver replica of the original trophy.

But, of all the many things that Vanderbilt brought to the game, it is the idea of vulnerability that appeals to me most. Alan Truscott, in the *New York Times Bridge Book*, describes a hand that Herbert Asquith (then Prime Minister) and Winston Churchill (then First Lord of the Admiralty) played while cruising the Mediterranean on board the Admiralty yacht *Enchantress* in 1912. Whenever he was short of a partner, Churchill would order one of his civil servants to the table. 'To cut with Winston,' so Herbert Asquith's daughter Violet Bonham-Carter later recalled, 'was to both his private secretaries a severe ordeal. Masterton was a really good bridge player and treated the game with respect. Moreover, though the stakes were low, he could not afford to lose overmuch. He used to sit in agony while Winston declared, doubled and redoubled with wild recklessness...'

On this occasion, Churchill was partnered by Sir Edward Marsh. There was the possibility of what is known as a 'Sandwich play', which describes the situation that arises when one's opponents' high cards in a suit are 'trapped' between a higher and lower card in one's own hands. The play is sometimes called a 'surrounding play', but I prefer the romance of 'sandwich' if only because it was so named in honour of the Earl of Sandwich, a previous occupant of the seat of First Lord of the Admiralty. In the hand in question, Marsh failed to spot the play, which meant that, instead of being restricted to eight tricks, the opposition went on to make eleven. Churchill was reported to have been furious and blamed his partner for making what was regarded as a 'normal' lead when defending in no trumps, which was the fourth highest card of his longest and strongest suit. In this case, Marsh had no honours in the suit, only the 9 7 6 2 of diamonds. Marsh duly led the two. Nowadays, with such cards most experts would lead the seven, because to lead the two is to suggest some honour strength. In this respect, as in so much else, Churchill was ahead of his time. But what holds my attention is the phrase Alan Truscott uses in partial explanation of the bidding on the hand. 'Nobody was vulnerable,' he writes, 'because nobody would be vulnerable until 1925.'

It was into this newly vulnerable world that Dad was born in the autumn of 1926.

13. Travels with Cal

I KNEW WHERE he was born: Kirkcaldy, on the northern shores of the Firth of Forth, and I knew when. But I had never been there. The opportunity to do so arose when a travel magazine commissioned me in the summer of 2003 to write an article about *Kidnapped* and David Balfour's flight across Scotland. My idea was to retrace his route, as it were, and in so doing to learn something of the place from which my father came. Even better, it was to be a father-and-son adventure. Sometime in early August of that year, Cal and I set off to Scotland to begin our quest.

We started on the small island of Earraid where David Balfour was shipwrecked and from where he set off to claim his inheritance. But Earraid has no hotels and so we took the ferry to Iona at the south-westernmost tip of Mull. Iona is now a pilgrimage site for Christians from around the world. Some come to spend time in the religious community that has now made its home in the old abbey first founded by St Columba in the eighth century. The story goes that Columba, who came of noble stock, had committed a grave offence by copying, without permission, a Psalter, which was therefore 'devalued'. After a pitched battle to recover the stolen copy (in which Columba prevailed), he was forced or decided of his own accord to leave Ireland and not to return until he had converted to Christianity the same 'number of souls' as had been lost in the battle over the book. The idea was that he would sail until he could no longer see 'home', settle there and continue his missionary work. He arrived on Iona with twelve followers and built his church.

Other visitors, like us, find themselves staying at one of the island's three hotels. After dinner, therefore, we settled ourselves in the pleasant and light lounge of the St Columba Hotel, watching shades of violet and mauve claim the distant horizons and toying with the pack of cards I had brought.

'We need two more to make a four,' said Cal with the confidence of someone who learned the game only months before. We looked about us for likely customers. The honeymoon couple in the corner were too wrapped up in themselves, but two elderly American women sipping tea looked a better prospect. Certainly, they were a better prospect than the group of four or five people pretending to listen to the large man telling them in a larger voice about his close relationship to Downing Street.

'You ask them,' I suggested, but this is never a battle parents can win, and so I eased over and asked whether the two elderly women played bridge and if so would they like to play a hand or two with us. Yes, they did play bridge, they replied, but, before they would answer the second question, both looked suspiciously past me to identify my proposed partner. I took this to mean that they had previously been robbed by smooth-talking cardsharps and weren't about to let it happen again. On seeing Cal, they readily agreed and soon we were seated around the table, cutting for partners.

There was some brief discussion of conventions, as there always is when strangers play bridge, the equivalent of establishing a common language. The metaphor doesn't quite work, for in bridge it is not necessary for opposing players to speak the same language or to use the same system in their bidding. It is enough only that each should understand the other's language. And the conventions are more than that, for it is not only about the bidding, but also about how you play the cards and what information your partner will gather from the choices you make. We agreed we would all play 'five card majors, a strong no trump, weak two bids, Stayman and Blackwood', which is the minimum one would expect when playing with Americans. All other bids were to be 'natural', which is to say that, if you bid, say, hearts, the opponents (and indeed your partner) could reasonably assume you had some of them.

'Bidding is the language of bridge,' says the ACBL site. 'The players, through bidding, decide whether the deal is to be played in no trump or in a particular trump suit. The dealer has the first chance to bid...'

With a pack of fifty-two cards there are something like fifty-three *octillion* possible deals. And yet there are only thirty-eight possible bids (1 to 7 of each suit and no trump; pass, double and redouble). It is not a lot. The number of bids is hopelessly inadequate to the task of describing so many possible deals. Over the years, different bids have taken on a complexity of meaning to cope with this. These bids – which say one thing but which may mean something quite different – are known as 'scientific bidding'. In this sort of bidding, each bid is invested with a variety of meanings depending on other factors – sequence, vulnerability, what the opponents have said and so on.

'A bid is a number combined with a word', the word refers to the suit or no trump in which the player hopes the contract will be played. The number refers to the number of tricks the partnership is willing to commit to over the book of six. 1 ♠ is a commitment to take 6 + 1 = 7 tricks, and a suggestion of spades as the trump suit. If 1 ♠ is the final bid, it would be the contract.'

This is all very well. At the 'one level', nothing very dramatic is going to happen. But what if you want to make a slam bid? How do you find out how many aces your partner has? You may have thirty-six points between the pair of you, but you're not going to make 7 ♥ if you're missing the ace of trumps. The most commonly known scientific bid is 'Blackwood'. It was invented by Easley Blackwood, an insurance salesman from Indianapolis (and later executive secretary of the American Contract Bridge League) who wrote to *The Bridge World* in 1935 with an article describing his newly devised system for 'checking' whether a 'slam' is available and therefore worth bidding. *The Bridge World* was controlled by Ely Culbertson and its endorsement could make or break a new convention. And Culbertson was very careful about whom he gave his endorsement to.

And bridge players had a problem. When a partnership had very strong hands and wanted to bid a slam, there was no easy system for establishing whether the partnership held key cards, particularly aces. Blackwood worked out a series of artificial bids that would enable one partner to 'count' the number of aces held. After you have agreed a suit, a bid of 4NT is 'asking for aces'.

A response of 5♣ means you have no aces, 5♦ means one ace, 5♥ means two aces and 5♠ means three aces. It is unlikely that your partners has no aces in his hand, but, in the circumstances that you have all four aces, you would also bid 5♣. In the event that the partnership is missing two aces, it is possible to settle in a final contract at the five level (requiring that eleven tricks be made) rather than 'go' for the slam.

Blackwood was a shy man. In his letter to *The Bridge World*, he asked that the convention be 'credited' to a pseudonym, Ernest Wormwood. Albert Morehead, who was editor at the time, initially declined to print Blackwood's article for the simple (and expedient) reason that 'our subscribers are too prone to accept anything printed in *The Bridge World* as a recommended change in the Culbertson system...' For three years, Culbertson continued to reject the Blackwood convention but, by 1938 (in a new edition of his *Gold Book*), Culbertson admitted that, even without his endorsement, it was gaining strength. Even so, it was not until 1949 that Culbertson acknowledged the superiority of the Blackwood Convention to his own system (known as Culbertson Four-Five) and announced to his subscribers that 'when a pair announced it was playing the Culbertson system, it should be assumed that the Blackwood Convention was being played'. Blackwood (the convention and the man) never looked back and it is now the most widely played (and widely understood) bridge convention.

The original version of Blackwood is still in use, although in recent years many players prefer an adaptation of it known as Roman Keycard Blackwood. In this case the king of the agreed trump suit is counted as a 'fifth' ace (or key card) and the response to 4NT of 5 ♣ usually shows zero or three key cards and 5 ♦ shows one or four key cards. This being bridge, of course, even this is not agreed and some partnerships 'do it the other ways round' with the 5 ♣ bid showing one or four key cards and the 5 ♦ showing zero or three.

Commenting on this story some years later, Blackwood framed it in political terms. 'Everybody was against me,' he said, 'but the people.'

Dad liked Blackwood, both the story and the bid. He too commonly felt that everyone was against him, not least the people. Although, of course, in our discussions we tended not to mention the people. There were too many of them and they were black, which made any conversations about popular support difficult.

But he liked the bid because it was clear and it worked.

On Iona we settled round a makeshift card table. 'Where did you learn to play?' Betty asked Cal.

'I always knew,' he replied with his trademark smile-and-side-ways-glance, an answer that he knew not to be true, but which charmed both them and me with its insouciant confidence.

'Always?' Mary asked.

'Ever since I was little,' Cal agreed. 'My dad taught me.' There was no suggestion from anyone that this might contradict his earlier assertion.

'When was that?'

'You won't remember, I don't think,' Cal replied.

'Well, then,' she replied. 'You had better deal.'

But Cal was suddenly overcome with shyness and it fell to me to deal the cards and make the first bid. Everybody deals differently. I think of my friend Mark who thumps every fourth card down like a man challenging for a duel or of the man at the club where I sometimes play who taps the top of each card as though trying to divine which it is. There are those who count each card as they deal it, those who talk as they deal and those for whom dealing is a reverential act, like painting the lines on a playing field or feeding a clean sheet of paper into the typewriter. For, at that moment, the moment before your cards are revealed, anything is possible. The stage is set, but the action has not yet begun.

We hadn't cut for partners. It seemed safer to assume that Cal would play with me and that our opponents would be Mary and her sister Betty from Toledo, Ohio. Mary was the elder, and the leader and it was she who regarded Cal shrewdly and calculated when the right moment was to ask our story and what brought us to this remote western corner of Scotland. She was pleased that I should phrase my explanation of our journey as a 'quest', and was delighted with Cal's rider.

'Also we get to eat whatever we like,' he said, which he knew to be only partially true but which he no doubt intended as a marker, lest I forget that travelling companions may have different agendas.

As dealer, I opened the bidding, and the game began while the shadows melted into the gentle evening air. Betty may have been the younger sister, but she was the better bridge player. She knew, for example, not to lead away from a tenace. Tenace is a lovely bridge concept. It means a situation where one hand has two high honour cards in a suit separated by two degrees. King and jack for example, or ace and queen. The word comes to us from the Latin 'tenax', meaning tongs. A tenace is weak if one has to lead from it, but strong if one's opponents have to lead up to it. Leading through it enables one to take a finesse. And Betty more-or-less 'counted the hand', which is to say that she not only looked at the cards in her hand, but used them and the bidding to work out what each of the other players must have held in their hands. It's a question of pattern. The most common pattern for a hand of thirteen cards is 4-4-3-2, which means that a player has two four-card suits, a tripleton and a doubleton. Other common patterns are 5-3-3-2 and 4-3-3-3 and these hands are known as 'balanced'. The more unbalanced a hand is, the less frequently that pattern will occur. A hand with 5-4-2-2 or 4-4-4-1 is slightly unbalanced – but a more frequent occurrence than a hand with 6-4-2-1 distribution. As Alan Truscott puts it, 'These patterns should become old friends. An inexperienced player should think about the pattern whenever he picks up a hand. He should reach the point at which an unfamiliar pattern will cause him to know immediately that he has the wrong number of cards: Somebody has dealt him 12 or 14.'

Neither Cal nor Mary 'counts' the hand. Cal bids with gay abandon. He is mindful of many tales of his grandfather's ability to conjure tricks from nothing (tales told entirely by his grandfather), and believes firmly, but wrongly, that bidding is only a phoney war before the real action begins. Mary, brought up in the 'proper' school of bridge, bids cautiously. Betty and I try to restore a little order to events. She overbids to compensate for Mary. I put on the brakes to avoid too much damage from Cal's wild calls. We adjust our play, but we do not try to 'correct' theirs. Both of us have read S.J. Simon's *Why You Lose at Bridge*. We know that it is hopeless to instruct your partner in the middle of a game. 'It can only confuse them. And there is no one more difficult to play with than a willing, but confused, partner.'

Cal does at least know that he must draw trumps, mindful of that oft-repeated mantra of his grandfather that 'there is many a man who walked the streets of London because he didn't draw trumps.' Cal has not yet been introduced to the world of money bridge and he does not therefore understand the connection between trumps and 'walking the streets'. But he does know that if you don't draw trumps you might lose some unexpected and inconvenient tricks.

We had played for little more than an hour by the time Cal fell asleep over the card table in the lounge of the St Columba Hotel on Iona and, although it was late, it was not yet dark. Summer evenings linger long in Scotland's western isles. Mary and Betty listened politely to our tales, but soon the conversation turned to Iona and the early Christian settlements there. Mary had been married at the abbey one summer after the war and thirty years later she and her husband renewed their vows there, and even now, ten years after his death, she returned every summer to the island where, she claimed, what held her was as much a quality of light as it was a question of memory. But, as we talked with the sudden familiarity of strangers, it became clear that what brought her back to Iona was not really the quality of the light, nor the memory of her husband, but an inexpressible longing to withdraw from what she knew into a place that corresponded, however roughly, with what she dreamed. And her dreams were filled with spaces in which the silence was the silence of a sea breeze in grass and the colours were smudged through the prism of great distances.

While Mary talked, Cal lay asleep in his chair, his blonde hair an unruly mop and his fingernails, I noticed with sudden concern, filthy with the grime of a day's travelling. Mary in any case seemed suddenly to tire of her memories. She nodded at Cal. 'You should put him to bed,' she said.

I said goodnight and lifted Cal from his chair to carry him through to our room. It was only when I laid him on the bed that I saw that he was still clutching the deck of cards with which we had earlier played the game he had always known, ever since he was little, way back, before memories begin.

The one he 'got from me'.

The morning after our bridge game in the St Columba Hotel, the sun rises bright and clear. It is the hottest summer on record and it seems clear that the day will be long and arduous. We rise early, breakfast and set off to catch a ferry back to 'the mainland', although it is actually the island of Mull. This was, according to David Balfour in *Kidnapped*, 'all bog, and brier, and big stone'. As we drive in our rented car along the single-track road, giving way every now and then to busloads of pilgrims to Iona, we see evidence that two and a half centuries of agriculture have left their mark. The bogs are gone. Instead, the hillsides are dotted with sheep and crossed by stone walls. In 1751, we're told, it was, 'infested with beggars'. We find only a pair of French hitchhikers to whom we give a lift. David Balfour walked the island without serious mishap in four days and arrived at Torosay on the northern shore 'far in better heart and health of body than [he] had been in the beginning'. These days, though, the ferry to Lochaline runs from a small dock at a place called Fishnish. While we waited for the ferry to arrive, I read a little from the book. 'In the mouth of Loch Aline,' David Balfour recalls, 'we found a great sea-going ship at anchor ... there began to come to our ears a great sound of mourning, the people on board and those on shore crying and lamenting to one another as to pierce the heart. Then I understood this was an emigrant ship bound for the American colonies.'

By this stage of our journey, I have told Cal many of the stories by which we account for ourselves – the sinking of his great-great-great-grandfather's (on my mother's side) ship, the *Annabella*, in

Durban Bay in 1857, his great-grandmother's travels in South Africa before her return to Scotland, my father's journey south to Cape Town in the autumn of 1940 and my own reverse journey into exile, overland from Cape Town to London twenty years ago. And I like to think he has some sense of the restless diaspora from which he comes. Even so, Cal doesn't see the problem. His journeys have always taken him home again. 'Why were they crying?' he asks. 'If they didn't like it, they could always come back.'

Well, not always. Sometimes you can never go back, I suggested, but Cal was having none of it.

'They could take a bus,' he says firmly.

'Your granddad didn't,' I say. 'He left Scotland when he was a kid and never really came back. He visited, of course, a few times. But he never came back.'

'Aren't they the same thing?'

'I don't think so.'

'I'll always come back,' he says, with the certainty of a child.

I wonder where he will go.

Cal and I follow the *Kidnapped* route through central Scotland. We fetch up, eventually, on the southern shores of the Forth. It was here, at the Hawes Inn at Queensferry, that David Balfour's uncle sold him into slavery, and the same inn, built originally in the seventeenth century, still stands. Now it is famous as a 'Kidnapped Location' and the sign above the door shows some suitably thuggish sailors belting an odd-looking David on the head with a cosh. Cal is more interested in the waters of the Forth brushing the foundations of the famous railway bridge. But I manage to get him to focus for a moment on what we have seen and where we have been.

'I like Scotland,' he says. 'But it's a bit scary. They remember everything.'

14. Remembering everything

My uncle Brian, Dad's youngest brother, has become the repository for the family memory. He lives near Edinburgh, not far from where they grew up. On a wet Sunday morning, he drives Cal and me north across the Forth River Bridge and on to Kirkcaldy. We're looking for the flat where Dad was born. The town is quiet when Brian, Cal and I arrive; there are few people about, perhaps because of the weather. The wind whipping in off the Forth means the town does not smell, as it sometimes does, of its most prominent industry, the manufacture of linoleum. Brian has done this journey once before and he more or less knows the way to the High Street. Here he has to pause before deciding we need to head towards the western end of the street, which is where we find the old building that was once the bank where my grandfather worked. Although it is now a jeweller's shop, the building appears not to have changed much. A covered arch leads through into a courtyard, from which a winding stair-case leads up the back of the building to the heavy old door of the flat. The current owner is not about and we are unable to go in. It was here, in the apartment above the bank, that my father was born into bridge's 'newly vulnerable world' in the autumn of 1926.

'He was born here?' Cal asks.

'Aye,' says Brian.

'And not in a hospital?'

'No,' says Brian, only he draws the syllable out in a character-istic Scottish manner.

'What, like in a bed?' Cal asks.

Brian and I nod solemnly. Cal thinks about this for a moment. 'It's hard to think of him as a child,' Cal says. 'I think of him as an old man.'

'Well, he was both,' Brian indulges him, 'sometimes simulta-neously.'

But the joke is lost on Cal who concentrates on counting the stairs that wind to the door behind which his grandfather was born. Brian – for whom Kirkcaldy was never home – looks about him with an air of wonder.

'You never lived here?' I ask.

He shakes his head. 'No. I was'nae born yet. But you can see why they left.'

'It's hard to imagine what it was like,' I say.

'You don't need to,' he replies. 'You need only think of his parents. His mother was his world. I'm not sure the rest mattered much.'

My grandparents soon left Kirkcaldy for the bright lights of Edinburgh. My grandfather had won promotion within the bank and this required him to move. On the strength of his advancement, they bought a small bungalow on the southern edge of the city, which is where they lived for the next forty-five years. There were five children in all. First my aunt Margaret and then Dad. He was followed at regular intervals by his three younger brothers, Robin, George and Brian.

I ask him what he remembers.

'Well, your grandmother was in charge,' he says. 'She ruled the roost. And as long as we remembered that – your grandfather included – we got along just fine. So the job with the bank took him to Edinburgh, but once she got there she never wanted to move again.'

I hardly knew my grandparents. We lived in South Africa. They lived in Edinburgh. But I did meet my grandfather once when I was nine and we travelled to Edinburgh at the end of a four-month

European tour. I remember only that his hair was whiter – which I had not thought possible – than my father's, that he too had a moustache which tickled when he hugged me and that his shoulders shook when he laughed.

On another occasion, Cal, Brian and I go to watch Scotland play Ireland at rugby. It is March 2005, a dismal time for Scottish rugby. The only question this season, as for some seasons past, is whether Italy or Scotland will end up bottom of the Six Nations championship. But today it is the Ireland game and so Murrayfield, the home of Scottish rugby, is full. Despite the freezing wind blowing off the Firth of Forth, the crowd is in good voice. Everybody knows Scotland is about to be thumped but it should at least 'be a good game'. And getting thumped by the Irish, while unpleasant, is considerably more palatable than getting thumped by the English. It is some years since Brian last attended an international match at Murrayfield, but it is clear from listening to him that it brings back many memories. In the thirties, my grandfather and 'the boys', the eldest of whom was my father, never missed a game. Their house was less than a mile from Murrayfield and, every time there was a 'home international', they would walk down the hill together to see the game.

Brian, Cal and I retrace the route through the streets of western Edinburgh to the stadium looming in the valley below.

'Was it always this cold?' Cal asks.

'Aye, I suppose it was,' Brian replies, 'although I don't remember it.'

At Murrayfield, Cal is unimpressed with his Scottish roots. The home team are being run ragged and their support barely gets above a whisper. By contrast, the Irish fans – who have great hopes for the first Irish 'grand slam' since 1949 and who in any case seem to outnumber the Scottish fans – are in full cry. Each successive attack is greeted with the melodic chants of 'Ireland, Ireland' and a waving mass of green.

'It would be better to be Irish,' Cal remarks.

'We can be Irish,' I joke. 'Your great-grandmother, Dad's mother, was half-Irish. That's how I came to be raised Catholic.'

For Cal, the idea of being 'raised anything' is a little remote, but he likes the idea of having Irish blood.

'Cool,' he says. 'I'll support Ireland.'

'No you bloody won't,' mutters Brian, sounding uncomfortably like my father. And to secure Cal's loyalties, we teach him a mildly ribald version of *Scotland the Brave*.

After dinner that evening, Brian produces a biscuit tin which – to my amusement – bears the legend 'perfect for the whole family'. It contains the family archive, such as it is, and includes perhaps thirty or forty photographs of my grandparents. I am struck by how little they seem to change, even though the photographs cover four or five decades of their lives. In each, the poses and expressions are the same. My grandfather is upright and correct, smiling cheerfully, looking regimental in dark suit and white shirt. When I remark on this, Brian says only that 'He looks like what he was, a bank manager.' My grandmother, in these pictures, is also very formal, but a little less accessible. Her smile is impatient, as perhaps she was with the photographer, and, even in the early pictures, one can sense her discomfort, for her legs cause her considerable pain. She stands very straight and her look is very direct, and her lips over the years have a certain compression to them. In this same collection, there are two photographs, one of each of them, taken on the same camera and on the same day, which must have preceded their marriage, and in which they are each seen to be cavorting in a park somewhere, playing, as my father would have put it, 'silly buggers'. I have no doubt that the phrase which came from him to me would have come similarly from his father to him. In this pair of pictures, my grandfather looks a little like one of the lesser Marx brothers, the one whose name one can never quite recall, whereas my grandmother reminds one more of a character in a novel, not the heroine exactly. She seems more like the one who brings about the downfall of the hero, perhaps inadvertently, though one cannot help but suspect malice.

'But that would be unfair,' Brian says. 'She was a tough old cookie, but your grandfather loved her dearly.'

'And Dad?'

'I'm not sure I follow?'

'Did he love them?'

'Ah,' says Brian. 'That's a different question. I suppose he did, at least until they sent him away.'

He says this only partly in jest.

Cal is confused. 'So Tom was born here,' he says, 'so why did he go to South Africa? Why didn't he stay?'

'He didn't have much choice,' I say.

'Not at first,' says Brian.

'He and George and Robin were sent to South Africa during the war,' I say.

'Why?' Cal wants to know. 'Was it safer?'

'I suppose it was, but I'm not sure that's why they did it.'

No diaries or letters exist to explain the decision that was taken in the winter of 1939–40 to send my father and two of his brothers to South Africa for the duration of the war. And my father never spoke of it, at least not to me. Perhaps it confused him too. Certainly, he was angry about it, both at the time and for many years to come. And he blamed his mother for it, rightly or wrongly.

Rose, the tough old cookie, rules the family. Throughout the thirties, the boys grow knowing that in the Balfour household the things that matter are faith and family and on both counts they answer to my grandmother. It is she who insists that they attend Mass and go to confession. It is she who supervises their schooling. It is she who maintains contact with the other family members, the myriad of aunts and uncles, cousins and grandparents who seem to proliferate all over southern Scotland. When, twenty years later, my mother is brought from South Africa to meet her future in-laws, she remembers it as an endless succession of meetings. 'I was under the impression that many of them were Balfours,' she wrote recently, 'though they were perhaps less numerous than the Quinns. (To this day I am not quite sure where they all fitted in.) Certainly, we went to see Tom senior's two sisters, Margaret and Janet, and his brother Hamish came round on more than one occasion to play bridge ...'

From their mother, the boys learn discipline and restraint. She teaches them the rules. From my grandfather, they learn something different. They learn to keep their own counsel and to communicate little. They learn to be private.

By the summer of 1939, their lives are full and stable. The talk of war affects them very little. My grandfather is too old for military service and the boys are too young. My grandfather works at the bank; my grandmother teaches at a college. Both banks and schools stay open during wartime. They see no danger to their lives or their jobs. Events elsewhere, which might mean Westminster or Windsor or Berlin, are just that: elsewhere.

Dad is the eldest of the boys and the most studious. He likes sport but it is not his passion. He loves books and, from his own telling of it, I have pieced together his reading during those early days. Some of it no doubt was read to him and some of it he devoured for himself, especially the Scottish canon: Buchan and Scott, Burns and Stevenson. *Prester John* and *Kidnapped* were favourites, to be read and reread until they were taken to heart almost in their entirety. I remember how, many years later, he read *Prester John* to me at bedtime and how towards the end of a chapter he would prematurely close the book and recite the last two or three lines from memory. He listens to the radio too, though he is not much interested in newspapers. He follows the build-up to war, but not avidly.

And, besides, it is summer. Across the garden fence there are the Braids, the open hills south of Edinburgh. They stretch out towards the Pentlands and it is here that the boys run free in scenes reminiscent of *A Child's Garden of Verses*.

It is Dad's golden moment, the summer of his thirteenth year. The holidays are spent with his cousins Betty and Rita on their farm in the Scottish Borders. In later years, my father will speak of these holidays as the happiest times of his life. There are salmon to catch and trout to guddle. There are moors to tramp and trees to climb. My father loves being outdoors. He loves the fresh wind in his face and the sea mist. He loves distant horizons and the illusion of freedom. He is carefree and strong and feels secure in the warm embrace of his family. To be sure, his mother is strict and his father a little distant, but he thinks this is true for everyone. Church is a chore and choir a bore, but so be it. He doesn't question the rules and takes his faith as it is presented to him.

Many years later, I recall Dad, in his chair by the window again, his pipe unlit on the stool, showing me the scar on the palm of his hand, which was not, as I might have guessed, a war wound, but one he had sustained while climbing a fence in order to escape the remonstrations of a neighbour from whose orchard he had attempted to steal a few apples. Whether this parable was intended to encourage or discourage us from such activities remains to this day unclear, for the suggestion of a grin played about the corners of my father's mouth even as he extracted from the tale its obvious moral. I remember how, in the telling of it, a wistful mist drifted across his eyes for, although all his life he had perfect vision, there was in his eyes an opaque, watery quality, like a man ever on the edge of tears that never came.

My great-uncle Willie comes by from time to time and, when he does, they bring out the cards. He taught their father and he might as well teach them. The way Uncle Willie teaches bridge is the same way the family has been taught the Catechism over the years. The basics are learned by rote, but what you do with them is entirely up to you. Just remember, you reap as you sow. And I have no doubt that the 'basics' Dad laid down for us when first he taught us bridge were the same 'basics' he imbibed when he was taught how to play by Uncle Willie and his parents. Like many of their generation, they had grown up with auction, but were quick to shift their allegiance to the new game of contract bridge now being universally marketed under the watchful and avaricious eye of one Ely Culbertson.

15. Man bites dog

Twenty-eight years after Dad was born, my parents met at that almost obsolete social event, the bridge evening, at the home of a mutual friend. My mother had recently returned from Europe where she had finished a year at the Sorbonne and where she had fallen 'more or less in love' (her words, not mine) with an American studying medicine. She planned to return soon to marry him. The details of the bridge evening are lost to time, but what I do know is that two days later my mother broke her back in a car accident. Travel to Europe was out of the question. When she awoke in hospital, swathed in a full-length body plaster cast, my grandmother told her that my father had called. He wanted to know if he could come and visit her. My mother said he could, and their courtship began. For the next fifty years, he liked to say that throughout their courtship Mum 'was plastered'.

Not all bridge evenings have such a happy outcome. In his *Hand of Bridge*, Barber spoke to the fears and experience of a vast class of people for whom bridge was a social lubricant in the era before television. His was imaginary, but some bridge stories are true. The most famous social game of bridge took place on an autumn evening in 1929. It was an uncertain time for many. Wall Street had peaked a few weeks previously, although many were either unaware or uncaring that this was the case. The stock market crash was still four weeks away. Financiers on Wall Street had yet to start defenestrating themselves.

Our story takes place in the home of John G. and Myrtle Bennett in Kansas City, Missouri. There is a cast of four. There is the perfume salesman, John G. Bennett, who is successfully advancing his career and the fortunes of the House of Richard Hudnut whose perfumes, compacts and *eaux de toilette* have lent a fragrant air to large swathes of the United States. And there are his wife Myrtle and their guests Charles and Mayme Hoffman.

Mrs Bennett – I struggle to think of her as Myrtle – was a formidable woman. She came from Arkansas and had first seen her future husband in a photograph at the house of a mutual acquaintance. Even then, and whether as a joke or not we do not know, she declared he was the one she would marry, and she made good this promise a year later by recognising him on the train, engaging him first in conversation and then in wedlock and moving with him to their newly appointed apartment in one of the finer parts of town.

Although by 1929 the Bennetts had been married for eleven years, they had no children (whether from choice or not, we do not know), and as befits childless couples of a certain income they had spent their Sunday playing golf with their friends. Towards evening, the weather turned and the couples decided it was too inclement to go as planned to the cinema. They would instead remain at home for what was known at the time as an 'ice-box supper' (which I take to mean that Mrs Bennett would not be overly taxed in the preparation of it) before settling down for a few rubbers of bridge. They agreed to play for table stakes of one-tenth of a cent per hundred, modest enough one would have thought to add a little something to the game, but not too high to cause anyone embarrassment when the reckoning came. At the trial – for there was a trial – Mayme Hoffman referred to them as 'fun stakes'.

On the evening in question, they played couple against couple, always a heady combination, and for the first hour or two all went smoothly. Luck went against the Hoffmans, and the Bennetts cooed at each other, as couples will when they are happy, in love and several thousand points to the good. But, as the evening wore on, their fortunes turned. Little has been written of it but one imagines also that they might have been a little drunk, for it was almost midnight when the fateful hand was dealt and that ice-box supper was already a distant memory. As is the way of these things, the cross-table conversation turned sour or, to put it more soberly, comments were coloured with the dye of constructive criticism. In the words of the lawyer and bridge historian, Rex Mackey, Mr Bennett himself dealt the fateful hand 'in a deal that became as legendary as the fateful Dead Man's Hand of Wild Bill Hickok. Neither the locale, the players nor the stakes – one-tenth of a cent per point – appeared to be laden with doom, yet so it proved.' As dealer, Bennett opened with a bid of 1 ♠. Mr Hoffman, to his left, overcalled 2 ♦, and Mrs Bennett leaped to 4 ♠. Whether she should have done so has been the subject of controversy ever since. Certainly, it was optimistic. A bid of 3 ♠ might have been wiser. But 4 ♠ was what she bid and that was the contract in which her husband had now to play the hand, for the bidding ended there.

Hoffman led and Mrs Bennett, as dummy, laid her hand on the table and retired to the kitchen where she began to prepare breakfast for her husband who was going early the next morning to St Joe. She returned to find that her husband had failed to make the contract and she proceeded to opine that he was 'a bum bridge player' and was heard 'to comment unfavourably on his parentage'. He for his part confined himself to suggesting that she had overbid, before slapping her at least once. At the trial, the Hoffmans proved in this and many other regards to be wholly unreliable witnesses, but we can be reasonably confident that Bennett then headed for the bathroom, perhaps to cool off, while his wife fell on the accommodating bosom of Mrs Hoffman, bewailing her misfortune and expressing the unforgettable but alarming view that 'No one but a cur would strike a woman in front of friends.'

It is the qualification that causes one to wonder.

Hoffman, perhaps wisely, confined himself to totting up their winnings and therefore was in no position to interrupt Mrs Bennett when she ceased wailing and disappeared into the bedroom from which she emerged carrying a Browning 9mm pistol. Four shots rang out. The first bullet went into the bathroom wall and the second into the lintel. The third and fourth lodged themselves in Mr Bennett, who promptly died.

The next day, the story made front-page news across the world. It became known, almost accurately, as the 'bridge table murder'.

Mrs Bennett was arrested, confessed and was charged with murder. But she soon recanted her confession and adopted the persona of a grieving widow and for the next months confined herself to making cryptic remarks like 'Nobody knows but me and my God why I did it.'

Fortunately for those who were interested in promoting the game of bridge, particularly Ely Culbertson, it took seventeen months for the case to come to trial. Its re-emergence on the front pages coincided with Culbertson's attempts to sell his new *Blue Book* on bridge. He was asked to participate in the trial as an expert witness and, having concocted a plausible hand for the occasion (for no actual records exist; those present were in no state to recollect exactly the distribution of the cards), he showed that the contract could have been made, and concluded that Bennett was, undoubtedly, 'a bum bridge player'.

This may or may not have helped Myrtle Bennett's cause. There are many bum bridge players in the world who do not necessarily deserve to be executed.

These were the hands, as subsequently put together by Culbertson:

NORTH

Myrtle Bennett

♠ A 10 6 3
♥ 10 8 5
♦ 4
♣ A 9 8 4 2

WEST

Charles Hoffman

♠ Q 7 2
♥ A J 3
♦ A Q 10 9 2
♣ J 6

EAST

Mayme Hoffman

♠ 4
♥ Q 9 4
♦ K J 7 6 3
♣ Q 7 5 3

SOUTH

John G. Bennett

♠ K J 9 8 5
♥ K 7 6 2
♦ 8 5
♣ K 10

If these were the cards, I have some sympathy with Mrs Bennett's view that her husband had bid a little optimistically, or 'opened light', as the more polite phrase puts it. To 'open light' is to start the bidding with a hand that is little more than average.

And yet, as Culbertson pointed out at the trial, the contract could be made. 'Mr Bennett had overbid his hand. Of that there can be no doubt, but even with this, so kind were the gods of distribution that he might have saved his life had he played his cards a little better.'

In any case, Mrs Bennett, advised by her ebullient defence counsel, Senator James A. Reed, was playing down 'the bridge angle' for all she was worth. Weeping copiously on the witness stand, she told how her only intention had been to pack the gun for Mr Bennett to take with him when he headed off for St Joe in the morning. Missouri appears to have been the kind of place where perfume salesmen routinely travelled armed and dangerous. According to Mrs Bennett, she had returned to the sitting room where she stumbled inadvertently over a misplaced chair, thus firing the first two shots. Mr Bennett, not unreasonably, misread her 'intentions' and thought she was trying to shoot him, either for being a 'bum player' or for hitting her like 'a cur'. He came out of the bathroom and tried to take the gun from her, in the course of which struggle she fired two more shots and fatally wounded her husband.

In his battle to persuade the jury that the whole thing was nothing more than a terrible accident, Senator Reed was aided by the fact that the story Mrs Bennett had told at the time of the incident, which differed markedly from the story she told at the trial, was excluded on technical grounds. Whether persuaded by her tears or by their grasp of the enormity of her husband's sin in not making the contract, we shall never know, but the jury went on to record a verdict of accidental death and Mrs Bennett went free. Perhaps their thinking was guided more by the mores of the times than by any consideration of forensic evidence or testimony. For, as one juror explained, 'She was only a woman, unused to guns. We reckoned that, if she'd really been trying to hit him, she would have missed.'

Quite what my father would have made of this story, I do not know. He would have wanted, of course, to know more about the hand, for the sin in his view would not have been to fail unnecessarily, but to have failed without style. Certainly, he would have had some sympathy with the assessment of Rex Mackey that it was not the Bennetts who were at fault on the hand, but the Hoffmans, who should have made a sacrifice bid of 5 ♦, thereby saving Bennett from his unfortunate demise. But what would undoubtedly have tickled him pink was that the jury verdict that Mr Bennett's death was an unfortunate accident meant the insurance policy taken to guard against his untimely demise was valid and Mrs Bennett, as sole beneficiary, was entitled to a cheque for $30,000 from a disbelieving insurance company.

The conclusion to the story is perhaps best told in the words of the great newspaper columnist Alexander Woolcott, for it is possibly apocryphal. Writing about the case in 1933 – it is to him that we owe many of the details of the aftermath – Woolcott says that Myrtle Bennett has not 'allowed her bridge to grow rusty, even though she occasionally encounters an inexplicable difficulty in finding a partner. Recently she took on one unacquainted with her story. Having made an impulsive bid, he put his hand down with some diffidence. "Partner," he said, "I'm afraid you'll want to shoot me for this."

'Mrs Bennett had the good taste to faint.'

16. The man who made contract bridge

THE EXTRAORDINARY THING is that the game the Bennetts played was less than four years old. That this murder should have been world news – that the *game* was world news – is largely due to the efforts of one man. Ely Culbertson, the 'Man who Made Contract Bridge', as his biographer John Clay calls him, came relatively late to the game. But, once he got there, he made it his own.

By his own account, Ely Culbertson first played auction bridge (though only briefly) in New York in 1912, but it would be some years before he decided it was the game through which he would make his fortune. He had first to live a life of extraordinary dissipation. He was born in Romania on 22 July 1891, the son of an American oil prospector and a woman whom he describes as 'a Cossack general's daughter'. 'My father's people were as American as the cigar-store Indian. My mother's people were as Russian as the giant and toothsome sturgeon that rush from the cold north down the many-mouthed Volga to lay their caviare in the great Caspian Lake.'

They lived in some luxury in the Chechen city of Grozny. Culbertson's formative years included a number of interludes that must have caused his parents some concern. He was, he says, at one time in danger of being executed as a revolutionary. Early love for a woman called Nadya – after whom he later named his daughter – drew him into the early proletarian struggles of the southern Caucasus. At sixteen, he was arrested and spent some months in prison with a number of revolutionary leaders who had been sentenced to death. It was one of these – a man named Ureniev who 'was my hero, my saint, my Socrates' – who taught him how to play chess and, more importantly, the finer points of *Vint*, one of the early forms of bridge.

The young Ely was wholly taken with his revolutionary mentor. He already considered himself to be a master of *Vint*, but Ureniev 'taught me principles I had never suspected', just as 'In life, he fired my imagination. He taught me how to translate the innocuous word "economics" into blood and thunder; how to distil reviving hope from black despair. He taught me how to think.'

Useful skills, no doubt, but it was his parents' interventions and the fact that he had an American passport that secured his release from prison. Ureniev was not so fortunate and, shortly before Culbertson's release, he was shot at dawn.

Culbertson's father had by this time made a considerable fortune in the oil fields of the Caucasus and increasingly devoted his time to promoting the musical career of Ely's younger brother, Sacha. Ely was left pretty much to his own devices, and started to travel. He read voraciously and he supported himself and a succession of lovers by gambling. By the beginning of the Great War, he was largely unemployable and largely self-educated and 'the erudition for which he was admired can principally be attributed to a self-imposed and invariable regime of reading a book designed to improve his knowledge for at least one hour before going to sleep each night. In this he was aided by an aptitude for languages. He conversed fluently in Russian, English, French, German, Czech, Spanish and Italian and had a reading knowledge of several others, including Latin and Classical Greek.'

In 1913, he decided to settle 'in the West' of the United States, and that *en route* he might as well 'get a few glimpses of Canada'. It was on this journey that he met the four playing 'a stupid game'. Soon after arriving in the United States, he left New York, heading for Canada. He spent time in the lumber camps until he was thrown out for being Bolshie. He made his way to California where he spent some time with the Mexican fruit pickers. In Fresno, he met a man named Johnson, an intellectual and stalwart of the Industrial Workers of the World, the so-called Wobblies. 'Johnson, a tender, kindly man was a bitter enemy of the tyranny of the state, and feared all forms of dictatorship. He believed in individualism, conceived and executed in freedom. He opposed the struggle of the survival of the fittest, and proposed free association of individuals in the spirit of co-operation. I was captivated by the essential sweetness of the anarchist doctrine. *It may be the system that will save humanity*, I said to myself, very much impressed by its sweep, depth of imagination and Christlike nobility.' These are the sorts of words with which he later speaks about bridge.

Such innocence! Such charm! Think what the world might look like now if he had chosen this form of politics rather than cards as the rock on which to build his considerable (but wildly varying) fortune. Culbertson was swept along on a wave of revolutionary fervour. But he was conscious that he lacked a theoretical base. In search of one, he 'dandified himself' and enrolled at Boone Preparatory School in Berkeley with a view to getting enough credits to enable him to enter Stanford University. There he was 'buried in books'. He learned 'Proudhon, Bakunin and Kropotkin by heart'. He was about to fall in love with a nightclub 'hostess' when both he and she were saved by the arrival on the international scene of Emiliano Zapata. Culbertson decided 'to leave immediately for Mexico, to study revolution in the flesh, so to speak, and help wherever I could'. Following what was by now a well-established pattern, he fell in love and was thrown in prison. The two were not necessarily connected.

But the Mexican revolution was confusing. Too many 'revolutionary saviours' appeared, each swearing that they and they alone would deliver the Promised Land. But as 'a "veteran" in the organisation of conspiracies', Culbertson was horrified by the 'lack of discipline, or system, and by the sloppy inefficiency of these "revolutionaries"'. And so he sailed for Havana, then Cadiz.

To read Culbertson's account of his youth is a strange and compelling experience. He was a natural storyteller, given to sweeping statements about others which were curiously revealing about himself. All the Mexicans wanted, apparently, was 'to get something to eat, to make love and to avoid back-breaking work', a charge which, I think, accurately describes the path of his own life up to this point.

Culbertson had 'a bad war'. When the United States 'entered' the war in 1916, Culbertson volunteered. He was too ill for active service and offered instead to act as an interpreter. It was 'the least he could do', and he was mortified when the US Army rejected him. He was perfectly fluent in many languages and had passed his examinations in all of them with distinction ... except English. 'It seemed my English lacked idiomatic flexibility, and betrayed a bizarre mixture of hobo and intellectual terms.' As a substitute, perhaps, for military service, he drank copiously, gambled wildly, read voluminously and fell recklessly in love. He started to hang out with the wrong crowd. 'I began to frequent certain Parisian cafés,' he writes, 'and private homes where I found small circles of people like myself – the disillusioned and the snobbishly egoistic.' These were people for whom the Marquis de Sade is a hero, and for whom no bookshelf was complete without a copy of de Quincy's *Confessions of an English Opium Eater*, and amongst such people Culbertson found temporary 'solace in a world of artificial lights and shadows'.

And then the war ended. So, according to Culbertson, did this cycle that 'had taken five miserable years to complete'. And with that – though I wonder at the simplicity of the decision – he decided to start again. He would support himself at cards, sufficient to fund his studies, and with a typical flourish he found someone with whom he could compare himself. 'Spinoza, I reflected, worked as a glass grinder four hours daily, earning enough to devote the rest of his time to studies. Why can't I do that with cards?' He started with poker, at which it was relatively easy for a man of his abilities to make money. He had soon accumulated enough to 'move over to a game of Plafond at the Café Régence', where the future British prime minister Andrew Bonar Law used to spend his time playing chess with Russian revolutionaries. There he made a bit of money, paid his debts and moved to London ... then Berlin ... then Riga ... then Brussels.

It is in Brussels that he came across the writings of Milton Work and made the 'interesting' discovery that some people in America were making good money teaching bridge. He decided to 'be the first bridge teacher in Europe' and placed advertisements in the papers. Strangely, the Belgian authorities took a dim view of this idea. They looked into his record, found traces of his supposedly revolutionary past and deported him.

Culbertson stands back to consider his situation. He has, he believes, little choice but to head for home, which he has by now decided is to be New York City. His father and brother are there, and he shares their apartment. It is 1921. He is thirty years old, with no job, no income and no qualifications. He falls in love, though not seriously, with an opera singer, through whom he meets other women of means and with plenty of time for leisure. They hire him to teach them about French literature. He is as surprised as anyone. 'The fee offered was two dollars a head – an enormous sum for me then, merely for talking about French literature. I became a teacher. I was brilliant, grave but devastatingly obscure... I toyed with the idea of marrying for money.'

And so on, and one detects in all Culbertson writes about himself the perfect training for the bridge player and salesman he was to become. Everything is an opportunity. Everything is possible. Wind and rain, sunshine and snow – all are the same for the bridge player, for one's success in the game depends not on whether you win or lose, but on how you cope with what you have. You are not playing the cards, but the people. For Culbertson, teaching French literature leads to teaching bridge – except that he and his new partner, a Mrs Shelton, have no pupils. Instead, they play with each other, and he teaches her the systems that have stood him so well in the salons and cafés of London, Paris, Brussels, Berlin and Riga. In the absence of clientele, they decide to pay a visit to the Knickerbocker Whist Club for an evening of duplicate bridge. In 1921, the Knickerbocker is as good as it gets. Everybody who is anybody plays there and anybody who plays there is somebody. Culbertson is determined to be a 'somebody'. Seeing 'a woman with a stranger', several regulars offer games at high stakes. Culbertson and Shelton win easily – more than a thousand dollars, so he says, and, when asked what system he plays, he says 'the Culbertson System'. 'It was the first time that my name was pronounced in a club. It sounded strange, hollow, absurd.'

Or so he claims. I suspect, actually, that it sounded completely thrilling. From that moment, Culbertson's name and his fortune were to be inseparable. His system was to be the 'Culbertson system'; his books were to be *Culbertson's Blue Book*, *Culbertson's Gold Book* and so on. He was that class of tycoon for whom business and self-promotion were the same thing and it began with him saying his name as often and as loudly as possible.

He becomes a regular of the Knickerbocker Club. After a short time, in which his winnings have reached more than one thousand dollars a month, he is invited to play 'on the third floor', the inner sanctum of the club where the best players congregate, amongst them Sidney Lenz and P. Hal Sims, the latter of whom Culbertson considers to be 'the best card player I ever knew'.

Also amongst them is Mrs Josephine Dillon, a bridge teacher regarded by many as 'America's greatest woman player'. Given her refinement, beauty, youth, brilliance and winning smile, I am not surprised to find that Culbertson is instantly in love. That she proceeds to take him to the cleaners on one particular hand in which she twice bids a suit in which she holds a void, and then proceeds to double him, only adds to her allure. He makes what is for him an uncharacteristic and possibly disingenuous admission: 'So captivating was her charm that even if she had not been physically attractive, it would have made no difference.' *I could fall in love with that woman*, he thinks, and the italics are his. Close readers of his memoir will know that all Culbertson asked before he fell in love was that the woman had a pulse and laughed at his jokes, but, in the case of 'Jo', it appears that the admiration was real. That she had already been married was a challenge rather than an obstacle. Her divorce, followed by her ex-husband's untimely death, had formed a 'cynical moat of bitter waters around her heart', and who better to storm them than Ely? All through the winter of 1921, he lays siege to her heart. He even shows her his voluminous diaries which, unsurprisingly, persuade her that he would be a dangerous man to marry. 'You could never be a *husband*,' she says, or, rather, he reports her as saying, as she leaves for Saratoga for the season.

But finally she succumbs. They marry, almost in secret, on 11 June 1922. He, of course, is no more employed or employable than he has ever been and their existence is precarious. Jo Culbertson teaches, Ely gambles and he continues 'to live in that twilight of frugal luxury which is an Eleusinian mystery to economists, toilers and tax collectors'. He thinks perhaps he will become a writer, but fears that this would be unwise and might 'jeopardise the material future' of 'a woman who had risked her life for me'. In an isolated attack of what one might call conscience, Culbertson decides 'to change'. His inner voices (he counts seven of them in all) appeal against the decision. 'So finally, after all these years, you've decided to become a bourgeois! Not even a rich one. Ely, listen to me; don't be a fool. Better be a gambler, better a bum, than to sell the best of yourself for money.' But the voice he called 'the Business Manager' wins this debate and a parliamentary compromise is reached. For ten years, he will devote himself exclusively to making money, to give Jo the 'home and stability I had promised'.

Jo is sceptical but enthusiastic. 'Special bridge cards were printed. They read ELY CULBERTSON, Bridge Instructor.' He planned it 'like a military campaign', for what he realised before anyone else was that it was not enough to be a teacher. He had to have something to teach, a system, a methodology that was recognisably his. Jo was already recognised as 'the greatest teacher in the country' (and not only by Ely), but she had only a few pupils and taught general principles of the game. All this is to change, though first there is work to be done. He writes articles for every publication, and he ghost-writes for every authority. He lets his name be mentioned, but no details be known. He becomes that most marketable commodity: a mystery. His name is everywhere, but nobody knows who he is or what, precisely, he does. When Jo asks him why he doesn't write his own book, he replies that there is no point writing a bridge book until you are famous. 'No matter how good it is, only a few thousand people will read it. It's like shooting sparrows with a howitzer. When I write my book the stage will be set for a big show, and I'll reach the multitudes.'

He sets about simplifying his system and its presentation. He also needs to establish himself as one of the best, for, as Rex Mackey says, 'Culbertson was not, by a long chalk, in the front rank of New York card players.' He is, however, a brilliant judge of people and he manages to attract to his team of four two of the greatest players of the time, Theodore Lightner and Waldemar von Zedtwitz. One sees it in this sketch of Lightner.

'He is gloomy and pessimistic, easily discouraged at first; but if things go from bad to worse he becomes a man of indomitable will, for then, having lost all hope, he starts to fight out of sheer spite.' It was Lightner who invented the 'Lightner double', the only double of a slam bid of which Skid Simon can bring himself to be approving. 'To my mind the Lightner slam double ranks as one of the most brilliant contributions to Contract Bridge yet made. It is simple. It is practically foolproof. It prevents partners who play it from making other, idiotic, slam doubles. And it is mathematically advantageous. I'll swap you all your Asking Bids for it, and throw in the Blackwood Four-Five no trump as well.'

The Culbertson four quickly establish themselves as the foremost auction bridge team in the country.

In 1926, the Culbertsons move for a time to California and set up a bridge salon at the Biltmore Hotel. They win $6,000 in a game with a casino operator who misjudges Jo's ability to play 'like a man' and for the first time their money worries disappear. Jo concentrates on teaching, Ely on business development. All the while they are still playing auction bridge. It is not until 1927, at a game in Santa Barbara, California, that Culbertson finally plays contract bridge. A new game. A game without experts or patrons. A game where the playing field is, for a brief moment, level. Culbertson is quick to recognise the possibilities here. He decides to make the game his own.

The couple return to New York where Culbertson's father is very ill. His father apologises to Culbertson that he has left him no fortune. His dying wish is that Ely, when he has a moment, should return to the Caucasus to prospect for oil. He had discovered what is, he is sure, a very rich oilfield, but until this moment he has told no one about it. He hands Ely a letter. The envelope is inscribed: *For Ely*. 'You will find all the instructions inside,' his father whispers. 'There is also a rough map.'

Culbertson completes the story, and with it that period of his life: 'We laid him to rest next to Mother. And we placed no tablet on his grave. As Jo and I rode from the cemetery, I felt a bulge in my coat pocket. It was Father's letter, containing the map. I had forgotten all about it. But in my heart he left an imperishable map revealing the secret treasures of human kindness and love – the map of his beautiful life.'

17. The square yard of freedom

DAD LEFT ME no parting gifts. Just a quick 'my regards to the kids' and 'the rest they will get from you'. Walking through our house of memories, I wonder what has happened to our card table. Mum has gone to sleep and it is too late to ask her, but David finds it tucked behind a door in the study. It is covered in burgundy felt, although I remember that, when we were learning, the felt was green. It is a standard table, made from mahogany, with four legs that fold out and a frame into which the felt-covered tabletop fits. It is a perfect space. Dad calls it his 'square yard of freedom'. It is a place where he can be free from the many claims that life makes on his attentions. It is his arena for excellence.

Bridge can, of course, be played without a table, but it's nice to have one. It lends an air of formality to proceedings. Morton

Sobell, the third accused in the Rosenberg espionage trial of 1951, was sentenced to thirty years' imprisonment. He describes how he and other inmates played bridge in Alcatraz prison in San Francisco Bay. On his very first day on Alcatraz, Sobell was invited to 'make a fourth', and it soon became a regular way to fill the hours. Playing cards was forbidden in many prisons, including the federal penitentiary in Atlanta, from which Sobell had been moved to Alcatraz. But on 'the Rock' it, 'was the only card game. We used a special deck of dominoes, rather than cards. They came in four colours to denote suits and the values were denoted by the number of dots: jack was 11 etc. And we had a wooden ledge for holding the dominoes so they could not be seen by others.' Not just a wooden ledge, but a card table too. The table was a 'blanket-covered folding-leg bridge table cut down to about 20 inches in height. We sat on hassocks.' Unfortunately, the bridge games had to share the yard with baseball games and the like, and 'on frequent occasions a softball would land in the middle of the table'.

But what impresses most about Sobell's recollection of the game on Alcatraz is its extraordinary capacity to pass the time. To commit to a game was to commit 'for the whole day' or 'frequently for the whole weekend'. 'With a population of 250 men it was not unusual to have 20 games going on weekends. It was a sight to behold: The men all bent over in their thin pea coats in the foggy drizzly cold playing all weekend long, about five or six hours each day. Usually the men arranged the game Friday night for a 25,000 or 50,000 point series. Whoever reached the figure first won. The bets were usually the moth-eaten stale Wings cigarettes which were distributed, three packs a week, to each man.'

Sobell was one of only a handful of 'political prisoners' on the island. Most were criminals with a history of escaping from other prisons. Most had never played bridge until they came to Alcatraz. But what impressed Sobell most was that 'each night, on return-ing to the cellhouse, many of the men would replay each of the hands from memory, discussing the bidding and the play.'

The ability to remember hands comes with experience, as well as with aptitude. Just as counting trumps is 'automatic' for expe-rienced players, so is remembering the lie of the cards and the key decisions, like what to lead, when to lead it. Each hand of bridge is a story. Character and plot are determined in advance. Cutting for partners determines who will play the hand. The deal decides with what. But the narrative unfolds only as each card is played, and, as we saw in Barber's operetta, the story is both physical and psychological.

Of course, some hands are hard to forget, because of the cards and the setting, or for the people who played them. I remember a story, for example, of a South African, Derrick Hirsch, who spent a large part of the Second World War in Japanese prisoner-of-war camps and who kept extensive records of the hands played. He was a passionate bridge player, referred to often as 'the driving force behind the amazing bridge organisation in one of the most festering camps in Siam'. Early on in the war, prisoners had to create packs of cards from anything that came to hand, just as Sobell and others did with dominoes on Alcatraz a decade later. But, as the war wore on, the Red Cross came to realise the popularity of bridge, and cards, scoring pads and even bridge books soon became a regular feature of Red Cross parcels. In an article in the *Contract Bridge Journal* in September 1947, J.G. Jordan described how bridge helped prisoners of war to stay sane. 'No other game could have assisted us so well,' he wrote. 'See that Colonel there? Couldn't play at all three years ago; watch him now with fierce intensity planning a pseudo-squeeze... In a word, bridge has become the principal means of keeping occupied the minds of half the camp, occupied against the ever-present menace of boredom which, behind the wire, is the forerunner of mental instability.'

Nowadays, we have computers for that sort of thing. Any duplicate bridge club will produce 'sheet hands' at the end of the evening so that one's hands are recorded for posterity. Perhaps this is helpful, if only to remind us that, while bridge may be a game of purposeful ambiguity, a game of bluff and double bluff, it is also a game of memory, tactics and probability. The mathematics of it are similar to poker, but a professional would rather play poker, because bridge is more risky – which is to say, more susceptible to chance. In part, this is because it involves playing with a partner. But bridge is also more technical. It requires mastery not only of probability and distribution, but also of the complex permutations of sequences of play. There are after all a little over 635 billion possible individual hands and 53,644,737,765,488,792,839,237,440,000 or 53 *octillion* possible full deals. And then there are several trillion more ways to bid them.

And yet individual hands remain in the memory. In his camp in the Far East, Derrick Hirsch suffered for his passion. One guard knocked out four of Hirsch's teeth with his rifle butt as punishment for playing bridge when he had been instructed not to. Despite this, a 'high point' of the year in camp was the 'international' match between Dutch PoWs and British PoWs. Coming from an ordinary shuffle was a deal so unlikely that even the guards were interested:

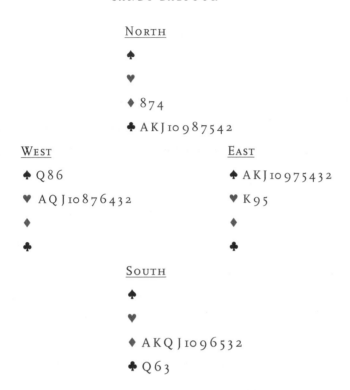

NORTH

♠

♥

♦ 8 7 4

♣ A K J 10 9 8 7 5 4 2

WEST

♠ Q 8 6

♥ A Q J 10 8 7 6 4 3 2

♦

♣

EAST

♠ A K J 10 9 7 5 4 3 2

♥ K 9 5

♦

♣

SOUTH

♠

♥

♦ A K Q J 10 9 6 5 3 2

♣ Q 6 3

This was 'tournament bridge' and so the hand was played twice. In one 'room', the Dutch held the East-West cards. In the other, the British held them. The Dutch quickly bid their cards to 7 ♥ and made all thirteen tricks. But the British pair had a misunderstanding in the bidding and ended up in a contract of 7NT. It was impossible for them ever to get the lead and the Dutch again won all thirteen tricks. As Andrew Ward points out in his guide to

Bridge's Strangest Hands, 'North-South had the minors and East-West had the majors. And who knows, they may even have had a major playing for them.'

Our bridge table carries with it a flood of memories. I realise I have probably never seen the legs in use. It was only ever the detachable top that came into play. It's to do with the geography of the rooms in our house. The dining room, with its huge old stinkwood table and upright *riempie* chairs, is a dark and Spartan place, dominated by a large Welsh dresser and hung with copper pots of varying vintage. The sitting room, by contrast, is bright and modern. It looks out on two sides to the lawn, the flat crown tree and beyond it what I invariably (though no doubt inaccurately) remember as a silver moon rising over the distant sea. The sitting room is a better place to play bridge, but it is a huge room. Around its edges are arrayed eight or nine chairs of differing degrees of comfort. My father, with his stool, his pipe, 'his' bookshelf with its ever-changing collection of pulp fiction culled weekly from the local library, his chair (and in later years the television remote) sits north-east. My mother (knitting, letters, crossword, books) sits south-west. The children move about the remaining chairs. When we play bridge, a small rosewood table is called into action. It opens up to reveal a surface that is marginally smaller in all dimensions than the playing surface of the bridge table. Unlike the bridge table, it is exactly the right height to play on while seated in an armchair. When we are about to play bridge then, the only question is whether to 'set up' in the north-east or south-west corner of the room. In either case, the bridge top is placed on the rosewood table and three other chairs are drawn around.

We find some cards and a scrap of paper to score on – depending on the state of rivalries in the house, it is usually enough for one person to score – and take our seats. Sometimes we cut for partners. More often, we take our usual seats, and Jackie and I fight over who is to shuffle. Dad interrupts by dealing himself.

The memories suddenly seem oppressive. Jackie watches me looking through the packs of cards.

'A bit sticky?' she asks with a smile.

I acknowledge the point. Dad had long, delicate hands, not surprising for someone who could play the piano. But he was clumsy too. Perhaps he was too tall or perhaps he had had too much to drink. When he had been drinking a little too much his dealing – though not his playing – would become ponderous and excessively deliberate.

'Are these new?' he would ask to cover himself. 'They feel a bit sticky.' A cold silence would hang in the room while we waited for our cards to be ready.

'Ah-tat-tat,' Dad would say, slapping our hands away if we reached for the cards too soon. 'Wait.'

It was rude to grab them too soon. It was also – which was more serious – detrimental to the interests of the game. What if there had been a misdeal? If someone had looked at their cards already, it would be too late to correct it. And so we wait as he places each card in turn, slowly, painfully, with a little click as his thumb snaps it on to the table. He raises his eyebrows as he deals and presses his lips together like a man on the edge of an announcement.

Jackie and I exchange glances. We're a little afraid to look at Mum, as though a glance will acknowledge too much. We're relieved when it's our turn to deal, even though Dad drums his fingers impatiently while we do it. Everybody who plays bridge deals in their own way. The first card is dealt to the person on the dealer's left. The last card is dealt to the dealer. Mum does it easily and quickly, finishing with a trademark scoop as she picks up her cards with the final card to be dealt. The cards that only a moment before were 'sticky' are suddenly smooth and easy to handle. Dad acts like he does not notice the discrepancy, but we know he does. He was never comfortable with his drinking.

Early on, I learned to count as I deal. Sometimes in fours and sometimes just straight through from one to fifty-two. Jackie is the quickest and the most precise. She slips the cards on to the table. They form neat piles in front of each player. When she's done, she sorts them quickly by suit and just as quickly she opens the bidding. 'One spade,' she says.

Dad doubles. Mum passes. What do I do? In bridge, this is called the 'takeout double'. It is a 100 per cent forcing bid. Unless I have about a million spades to the ace (unlikely, given that Jackie's opening bid has shown she has five), I cannot pass. I have to say something – but what? Dad's bid means he has a strong hand and at least three cards in all the other suits. It also suggests he doesn't have many spades. Most likely he is strong in hearts. What it does not do is suggest that we can defeat a contract in spades – unless I have a whole bunch of them. According to the *Encyclopaedia of Bridge*, the takeout double was invented 'by Major Charles Patton in New York and Bryant McCampbell in St Louis in 1912–13'. It was originally called a 'negative double' and later – after it was introduced to tournament play as part of the Roth–Stone system – a 'Sputnik Double', apparently because the Russian satellite went into orbit at the same time.

In our family, we play the negative double. I have to say something. With a very weak hand, I choose the smallest suit bid possible. If I have a moderately weak hand, I might bid one no trump. With a strong hand I have more choices.

On this particular occasion, I have a hand worth absolutely nothing – except that I have a void in hearts. Reluctantly I bid 2 ♣. Jackie bids 2 ♠ and Dad overcalls with 5 ♣. Mum doubles – this is for penalties, not for takeout. She is, with some justification, expecting me not to make the contract. Everybody else passes. Since I bid the clubs first, I have to play the hand. Jackie leads the ace of spades – meaning she has the king as well – and Dad tables his hand.

We go one down. I am able to use my void in hearts and Dad's void in spades to cross-trump eight tricks. Dad has two high diamond honours, which gives us ten tricks. There is nothing I can do about the fact that Mum has the A-K-Q of clubs.

Dad is delighted. 'One down is good bridge,' he says.

18. The game goes global

ELY AND Jo Culbertson are planning a family and he realises that he can no longer rely on gambling for his living. He needs something a little more reliable. He needs a plan. Typically, he has one.

'You see, Jo dearest,' he says to her, 'if we are to make fifty thousand dollars a year as the leading authorities in contract bridge, we must be known to millions. That will take us about ten years. Of course, if we're lucky, we may do it in five or six, but we'll have to be mighty lucky. We're handicapped by lack of money. However, that's unimportant, since my plan is absolutely scientific.'

It actually took less than three years for Culbertson to become both famous and rich – and it had much less to do with luck and everything to do with Culbertson's extraordinary abilities, the least of which was at the bridge table. His plan was outrageous and simple: by engaging in every area in which he might attract public attention, he would turn himself into a celebrity – into an 'American Idol', as he put it, seventy-five years before the television programme of the same name. And he would then use his celebrity to sell anything and everything that can be associated with bridge. But even he struggled to keep up with the spread of contract bridge. 'The Winter months raced by. Contract bridge, begun by half a dozen players in 1926, had grown to a stream by 1927, a river in 1928, a torrent in 1929 and until now, in early 1930 it looked like a tidal wave.'

Among his many talents is an ability to keep a metaphor going, even if he is prone to sweeping exaggerations: 'Daily, at least ten thousand players changed from auction to contract, and all of them learning our name and our system.'

And he knows that all of them need an authoritative voice to keep them abreast of developments in the game. After a series of unsatisfactory negotiations with publishers, he decides to publish his own magazine. He launches *The Bridge World*, which remains the leading bridge magazine today, and hires a staff. From time to time, he is unable to meet the payroll, but he persists – and his staff remain loyal. He gets into the cruise business, supplying 'accredited' teachers to The French Line shipping company. And, crucially, he resists all pressure to publish a book. They must wait, he insists every time someone suggests he write it. They must wait.

But what he really means is '*We* must wait' – wait until 'we' are famous, until our names are known by millions. He continues with his preparations. 'I gave free lessons… I broadcast on the radio – free of charge. I gave free lectures. I buttonholed everyone I could meet… In every letter and every speech I told them of my forthcoming work – the *Blue Book*.'

And then he is twice lucky. First, the great bridge murder comes to trial and he appears as an expert witness. The lachrymose Mrs Bennett is front-page news for weeks, and Culbertson is happy to join her there. But – more importantly – he receives a challenge from a Lt Colonel Buller of England who claims that a good English bridge team will beat any American one. Culbertson accepts the challenge and a date is set for the match to take place in London. In the heady days before leaving for London, he finally dictates the *Blue Book*. He – perhaps not surprisingly – gets stomach ulcers from the stress. At one stage, he is rushed to hospital. After surgery, he continues a punishing regime of dictating to a relay of secretaries for eighteen hours a day. Fortunately, he has Jo to do the difficult work. She checks the proofs and supervises production. The last chapter is dictated in the taxi to the New York harbour. He boards the ship and from the dockside his publisher, Lewis Copeland, shouts out a question: 'How about a dedication?'

'To my wife and favourite partner,' Culbertson replies.

Sales are phenomenal. The first print run is 6,000, of which 4,000 have been bought in advance by subscribers to *The Bridge World*. On his arrival in London, a cable from New York greets Culbertson:

> BLUE BOOK OUT STOP FIRST EDITION SOLD
> OUT TWENTY-FOUR HOURS STOP SECOND
> THIRD EDITIONS NOW PRINTING ALSO SOLD
> OUT SUCCESS ENORMOUS STOP YOU ARE RICH

But still he and Jo could not relax. Defeat at the hands of Colonel Buller and his team could kill the sales of the *Blue Book*. To succeed, his system had to be seen to be working. Fortunately, the Buller methods were inferior to the Americans', although, as many analysts have since pointed out, both systems left much to be desired. Rex Mackey quotes one hand in which Jo Culbertson drags her English opponents into a cast-iron game of 4 ♥ , 'which neither wishes to bid. Then, to add a bonus to her generosity, she doubles them. And this was the match that made Culbertson famous!'

And famous he was. An international celebrity ready and willing to cash in on his fame. The old guard – those like Whitehead and Work, Sidney Lenz and Albert Reith, who had made their names before contract bridge was created – realised they had to respond. They formed the 'Official Group' and published 'The Official System of Contract Bridge' under the aegis of the 'Advisory Council of Bridge Headquarters Inc.' But Culbertson was ready to take them on. Before and after a whirlwind tour of Europe he issued a series of challenges to the Official Group. He was prepared to play them 'anywhere, any time for any stakes they chose'. After much goading by Culbertson, Lenz reluctantly accepted the challenge.

Culbertson knew that 'if the Buller contest was the foundation of his fortunes, defeat this time would be their ruination', but in choosing Lenz he chose well, for Sidney Horatio Lenz was no less a character than himself. He made his millions in the timber industry and retired when he was thirty-five. He joined the Magic Circle, was US draughts and table-tennis champion for many years and played tennis and golf competitively with the very best. Lenz did not particularly want this 'battle' with Culbertson. He had nothing to gain from it; his fortune did not depend on bridge. But what he had not calculated was that Culbertson had everything to lose. And so the stage was set. The 'bridge battle of the century' would take place in New York City in December 1931 and everyone in the world would know about it – if only because Culbertson took the unusual but highly effective step of giving bridge lessons to a group of media moguls, including the then President of the Bell Newspaper syndicate. He made sure they understood the story – that he and Jo were the young innocents struggling to free themselves from the oppressive old guard represented by Lenz. Lenz had chosen Oswald Jacoby as his partner. The stage was set for Culbertson's greatest triumph – or his greatest defeat. Even the *New York Times* called it the 'sports event of the year' and, looking back through the newspapers of the time, it seems that only two important events occurred in the United States that month. There was a presidential election, won by one Frank Delano Roosevelt, and there was a bridge game at the Chatham Hotel.

But for the moment Ely had to concentrate on the play and not on the extraordinary spectacle of bank presidents and actresses, bishops and publishers queuing to glimpse for a moment the great Culbertson at play. The *America Mercury* gives a good feeling of the mood in the hotel:

> After minutes of unbearable suspense, the first
> messenger burst forth, panting and breathless with the

world-shaking communiqué: Mr Lenz wins the cut and sits down in the North seat. The first words of the match were spoken by Mrs Culbertson. They are, 'Where do you wish to sit, Ely?' Telegraph instruments start flashing this piece of news to the farthest outposts of civilisation. Copyists, scribbling frantically, distributed copies of the hands to the throngs milling about in the corridors and lobby. In the room set aside for the working press, reporters phoned in the news. Hot upon the heels of the first message came another: Mr Lenz and Mr Jacoby get the contract on the first hand at three no trumps. Flash! Lenz and Mr Jacoby win the first rubber amid some of the most terrible bridge ever played by experts.

Culbertson called it 'the greatest peep show in history'. His team won a total of 122,925 points and seventy-seven rubbers compared to Lenz who won 113,945 points and seventy-three rubbers. It was very close, but the scale of the victory mattered to Culbertson not one jot. His point was made and his fortune would be secure. He had millions of converts around the world. That the Official System was actually better was neither here nor there. As Alan Truscott notes, 'With hindsight, the Official System theorists were generally right and the Culbertson was generally

wrong, but Culbertson had the ear of the public ... in two important areas, valuation and the opening bid with game-going hands,
the verdict of history has favoured Culbertson's rivals. But nobody
read their book.'

Everybody read Ely's book. They read *Blue Book* in its many editions and, when the *Gold Book* supplanted it, they read that too.
And, while they were at it, they read his magazine and Jo's books.
They read the little booklets he prepared for Chesterfield cigarettes and which the tobacco company distributed 'free' with every
pack of cigarettes sold, and they read the wrappers on Wrigley's
Chewing Gum, on which were printed extracts from the
Culbertson systems. They watched his movies – he made a quick
run of six films for RKO Studios – and they listened to his teachers who now numbered more than 10,000. The RKO features,
Mackey notes, may not have 'made cinema history, but they made
money'. It could easily not have been the case. By Culbertson's
account, 'they sent a director, a scenarist [sic] and a gag-man from
Hollywood to help me prepare the scripts. The gag-man decided
to reverse the usual order in dealing and bidding. His theory was
that what we needed in the pictures was the unusual, and that
this would be funny. The director wanted a scene in which three
southern ladies, looking for a 'fourth', pounced on a Negro butler.
I wanted them all to go back to California ...'

Culbertson's articles were syndicated to more than 150 American and foreign newspapers. Jo's were in all the papers belonging to the Hearst Corporation. With typical panache, Culbertson gives this view of the aftermath of the 'bridge battle of the century': 'The show was over. We won millions of new friends. We were world famous. *And we were ruined!* We had barely enough money for a one-week trip to Havana and back.'

The italics are his, but I can't help thinking that, if he was 'ruined', it was a form of ruination devoutly to be wished. While paying for the 'lobster-Newburg-lines of society people that I fed in the long corridor of the Chatham' may have created a temporary cash-flow problem, his fortune was secure. The *Blue Book* and the Culbertson's *Summary of Contract Bridge* sold in vast numbers and many languages. A Braille edition was produced. 'They found their way into lumber camps, hospitals, and, appropriately, asylums. It is a fact that there was a near riot in Sing-Sing between two student groups who disagreed as to the correct system bid.' All over America, and all over the world, the people read his books. They may have learned lousy bridge, but they loved it.

Not least in the southern streets of Edinburgh where the *Blue Book* and its wisdom were fed, piecemeal and then wholesale, to my father and his brothers. By the winter of 1939, bridge had taken a firm grip on the routines of the family where its many virtues are extolled weekly. My grandparents, like many of their generation, took it to be self-evident that bridge represented all that is wholesome. They would without question have echoed the views of Somerset Maugham who was, as we have seen, a fanatical bridge player. The successful player, he wrote, will be 'truthful, clear-headed, considerate and prudent; these are also the essentials for the more important game of Life.' And while it may be sad, as Rex Mackey put it, 'to see the master of cynicism dipping his pen in golden syrup', the idea that bridge somehow represented something good had taken hold. Nor did it appear to matter, as Mackey commented, that the enduring popularity of bridge could be 'largely ascribed to its appeal to practically everyone [sic] of the baser human instincts'.

Mackey justifies this extravagant view by examining some of the motivations that 'impel its devotees to play, think, talk and live duplicate bridge year in and year out...' Perhaps, he begins, neither St Augustine nor St Thomas had bridge in mind when they placed Pride at the top of the list of Seven Deadly Sins, but they should have. For 'no other product of human ingenuity has given the ordinary man greater opportunities to indulge in a vanity he is otherwise compelled to disguise.' Well, indeed. But the theology of the Balfour household takes a benign view of pride. Effortless superiority is the ideal, but mere superiority will do and one should be proud of it. And this particular form of pride comes cheap. Even to play in the clubs will cost only half a crown or so, and at home it is free. Not even the deal in which Culbertson sold Kem, his playing-card company, to a group of German investors made it expensive to play the game. Of all the deals he did, and there were many, this is the one that he most liked to boast about. After a year of 'psychological manoeuvres and counter-manoeuvres', the investors offered to buy the company (then trading at a loss) for three hundred thousand dollars. This was 1937 and Culbertson was going through one of his lean periods. 'Take the money and run,' said all those around him. 'Not a chance,' said Culbertson. More fencing followed and more time passed. Culbertson turned down four hundred thousand and then half a million dollars. Eventually he agreed a price: six hundred thousand and ...

'So! Is there an 'and'?'

'Yes. You'll want to make use of my name and experience, won't you?'

'Of course. But we won't pay a cent more than our offer.'

'That's your business. But I would be doing injury to my business genius [by all accounts he really spoke like this] and glorious name if I took less than five percent gross on all the money received by you.'

'For one year?'

'No,' I said blandly, 'for fifteen years.'

In the event Culbertson wasn't finished. The deal only gave the buyers the American rights. The 'world' would cost them more. The buyers walked out, but Culbertson knew they would be back. 'The road they have yet to travel, I thought, is very much shorter than that which they have travelled already. They'll come around.'

And they did. We all did.

19. Bloody Culbertson

BY THE END of the decade, when my father learned bridge, there was no authority other than Culbertson. A distinctively British style of play had yet to emerge. One was in preparation, being tried and tested by a brilliant group of men in London – but the war would interrupt their efforts. For the moment, Culbertson was bridge and bridge was Culbertson.

'Oh, Culbertson of course,' said my uncle George, when I asked him who had guided the hands of the family when they learned bridge. 'Definitely Culbertson. The *Blue Book*. It was always the bloody *Blue Book*. Took me years to recover.' George is the only living witness to my father's journey to South Africa and it is he who gives me some sense of what it was like.

After the golden summer, the autumn of 1939 comes coldly to

the Balfour household in Greenbank Road, Edinburgh. According to my uncle George, a new reality takes hold. Perhaps as the eldest son Dad feels it more than his brothers. He is thirteen, old enough to be thinking about what he might do with his life. Old enough to think about the wider world. The radio is on in the corner with its incessant news of war, and yet he finds the war uninteresting. He is more interested in the physical world. He wants to know how and why things work the way they do. He likes systems and rules. He likes things to be predictable. He dislikes – distrusts – emotion. I am not surprised to learn that, when his uncle Willie presents him with a perfect world, the world of bridge, he takes to it with ease and delight.

Certainly, it helps to pass the long evenings.

But the way George describes it, it is clear there are also tensions in the house and long periods of silence. My grandfather turns down a promotion, which would have meant moving from their house in Edinburgh to some smaller city. And another disaster has struck. My grandmother is found to have a malignant tumour in her leg. There is no option but to amputate. She agrees and the operation is performed. They give her a prosthetic limb, but things will never be the same. Her leg causes her great grief and she compensates through an excess of zeal in disciplining the children. Even so, the boys seem a little beyond her and so she is excessively harsh on my aunt, Margaret, who is by this time sixteen years old. Margaret becomes a surrogate mother to the boys.

My grandparents try to maintain the appearance of normality. Their faith remains strong and their politics remain conservative. They disapprove of Hitler, but fear socialism and communism. They despair at the revolutions of the east. They wonder what to do with the children.

For the fact is that home is becoming an uncomfortable place to be. The war, the distant war, has settled on Britain like a dark fog. Christmas has come and gone and hostilities have hardly commenced, let alone ended. And even that is not really the issue. The real difficulty lies at home where Rose takes out her anger at her disability on anything and everyone around her. There is a suggestion – though heaven help anyone who articulates it – that my grandmother cannot quite cope, and I am not surprised. Although the house is a bungalow, it lies on a steep hill and there are many steps about. Even with her new prosthetic leg, the shortest journey must have been a great effort. My grandparents, no doubt, are drinking a little more than they should each evening. Tempers are easily frayed. The easy domestic rhythms of the preceding decade have been broken. For a family so determinedly focused on its own affairs, the war seems an impertinence they are powerless to prevent.

There is one possibility that might help. They could send 'the boys' away for the duration of the war. One of Rose's oldest friends, who is known within the family as 'Nelly Bell', has settled in South Africa where she is a highly successful school headmistress. She writes to suggest that the boys be sent to her. She will take care of their education. Tom and Rose should not worry. Bursaries and scholarships are available and she will take care of any shortfall. There are good Catholic schools; it will be perfect for the boys. They corresponded often and Nelly Bell would have been fulsome in her praise of the beneficial effects on young minds of a colonial upbringing, where boys especially had the space to run free and would learn how to be men free from the constraints of class that so hampered those who grew up in Britain.

My grandparents debate this. The advantages both for them and the boys are obvious. South Africa, land of plenty, land of sunshine, will be good for them. They will get away from the war. Their going will ease the burden on my grandmother. Nelly Bell will take care of them. The disadvantages are less obvious and easy to gloss over. And so, after a time of debate, the decision is made. The boys will be sent to South Africa to attend St Aidan's College, a Jesuit school, in Grahamstown. It is only the three boys. Margaret, my aunt and the eldest child, must remain at home to help her mother. And Brian, the youngest, is only three years old and too young to be sent away. And so the decision is made; the boys are to go to South Africa.

South Africa is, in any case, not as distant or as scary as it might have been for other families. As a child, Rose had spent some time there when her father went to seek (and found) his fortune, but it was not a place of which she had fond memories. Her parents parted company early. The story is that my great-grandmother made it as far as the railway junction of de Aar in the northern Cape before she turned back, disgusted by the heat and the dust, the rough and ready nature of what was still frontier life. She returned with Rose first to Ireland and then to Scotland where money from the gold mines paid for her to attend a respectable series of boarding schools. But after she left school the money stopped. She and her mother were not 'in the inheriting line'. She would have to earn her own way, which she did through teaching.

Once the decision is made, three metal trunks are purchased, one for each boy, and in the weeks preceding their departure the trunks stand in the sitting room. The trunks become a symbol of the journey. They promise adventure and excitement and something new, and everybody learns to ignore the clang when they close, like the sound of prison bars slamming shut.

Rose watches silently while the boys make stencils and paint their names on each trunk.

It seems curious to me that in the photograph taken to record this momentous departure there is no look of fear or concern on my father's face, only a mildly amused curiosity that his parents are bothering with this visit to the photographer's studio. My father, the eldest and tallest by a distance, sits in the middle. To his right is Robin, the second son, who could have picked a fight in an empty house and whose temper would in future years become the stuff if not of legend exactly, then at least of considerable concern. And to his left is George, the youngest of the three travellers. Even then, George looks diffident and shy, intelligent but a little nervous, as though he alone of the three has some sense of what is to come. For look at Tom and Robin. Tom has his arm about each brother, but on the second glance I can see that his fingers are curled round and digging into the soft spot just below Robin's kidneys. And, on seeing this, I realise why Robin is wearing an expression of suppressed comic outrage and why, indeed, he is holding his arms in such a manner as to deliver with his left elbow a short sharp jab to my father's ribs.

For the younger boys, then, this is something of an adventure and both my surviving uncles confirm that for days and weeks and months before the departure their great tin trunks stood in the bay window of the house in Greenbank Road and gradually filled up with the accoutrements that would be required for the journey and for the months to come. Telegrams are exchanged with Nelly Bell. Will they need coats? Hats? They go on shopping expeditions and make lists. Things are put in the trunks and taken out again.

At the same time, Dad is uneasy in these newly shifting sands. Nothing seems to hold. The bedrock of family, church and school is ripped up without so much as a by-your-leave. 'It is for the best,' his father assures him. 'It will make you a man,' says Rose, which I think he suspected to be true, but on the surface he chose not to believe either of them. He bears the burden of responsibility. He is old enough to know that this is not just an adventure. Then, and for the rest of his life, he feels betrayed: by his mother for making the decision, and by his father for acquiescing to it. He feels powerless – needless to say, 'the boys' were not consulted in this decision. He feels alone; both his mother and father admonish him repeatedly to look after 'the little ones'. Despite reaching puberty, he is not yet ready to renounce his claims to be a boy. But no one is charged with looking after him. It was too late. Like it or not, he was the man of the party and he was expected to behave like one.

The day comes for them to leave. They 'get out' just in time, sailing from Glasgow on the *City of Paris*. The Blitz on Britain's provincial cities is about to begin. The boys are a little scared, but they hide it well.

'It is,' so my uncle George says as his parting shot to his mother on the day of their departure, 'the best day of my life.'

Dad says nothing. He has learned to hold his tongue. He is not yet fourteen but it will be nine years before he sees his parents again.

20. Freetown

THEY HEAD WEST, for there are U-boats about. The route from Glasgow takes them 'as close to Iceland as we could get without hitting it', before they turn south to travel in more or less a straight line through the Atlantic. Every day on board there are rumours. A U-boat has been sighted a few miles off the port bow. Another ship has been sunk and gone down with all hands. There are forty-five other children on board, including my uncles Robin and George, and four or five times as many servicemen who are being despatched to South Africa or Aden. One morning, they wake to find the engines thundering. A tannoy announcement informs all on board that this time it is for real; they are taking evasive action and are to stand by for further information.

According to George, it is a mix of the thrilling and the banal. They tighten the straps on their lifejackets and try to see what is happening. Their chaperones tell them to stay still and keep their heads down. Minutes pass… but 'nothing happens'. They find themselves instead with a damaged engine because the captain had pushed the ship too hard for too long in his efforts to avoid the U-boats. But at least they are clear of U-boat range. They turn west again, and for several days they limp across the glassy ocean before pulling into Freetown, Sierra Leone, for repairs. Here the ship is besieged by traders offering all kinds of goods for sale or exchange. The children are warned not to talk to them, nor to buy anything. It is here that my uncle has his one clear memory of the journey, for my father, in a characteristic display of enterprise and *droit de seigneur*, takes it upon himself to trade his brother's slippers (purchased only a few short weeks before at the Marks and Spencer store in Princes Street) for three dozen mangoes, as a consequence of which the boys are all violently sick and to a man forswear mangoes (and indeed most fruit) for the rest of their lives. When not 'fencing stolen goods' (as George puts it), Dad plays on the deck or reads, or watches the passing waves, no doubt with a mix of pleasure and tedium. From his trunk, he draws a pack of cards and tries to engage others – soldiers, too – in games of bridge. In this he is mostly unsuccessful for they wish to play for money and reckon (rightly) that my father will not provide them with sufficient wealth to merit the indignity of being seen to fleece a mere boy.

I have read of games of bridge played on the interminable journeys in defence of one part of the Empire or another. Private Stanley Anderson, for example, who was wounded by shrapnel on 22 July 1944, recalls playing bridge on his troopship home across the Atlantic. He had just made up a four '(even though none of us knew how to keep score) when the ship's PA system came alive with the news that the war in Europe was over.' They feared it might be a rumour or a sick joke, but 'when we were issued two bottles of beer each, we had to believe it must be true.'

Troops or no troops, my father has his brothers to teach and, while Robin shows a stubborn reluctance to engage, George is a willing student and happy hours pass crouched over the pack of cards and a tattered copy of the *Blue Book*.

It's not always easy. There are periodic alarms, and they have to wear their lifejackets at all times. At night, the lifejackets are next to them in their bunk beds. There are lifeboat drills to practise – one passenger recalls that, after a week, they had got it so that all children would be in the lifeboats in less than three minutes. Before reaching Freetown, they are all dosed with quinine to prevent malaria, which is 'foul', and have to 'smear themselves with ointment' if they go out after sunset as a guard against mosquitoes and other insects. Every morning, they have lectures from their government-appointed chaperone on 'travel, South Africa and divinity', and one imagines my father would have thought he knew all there was to know about two of the three. South Africa, in the imagination of the boys, looms large, informed by the long list of Victorian writers and especially by Buchan and Kipling.

South of Freetown, they stay closer to the African coast. My father must have marvelled at the deep brown of the waters that surround the mouth of the River Congo. I have read, for instance, of the wonder it caused Joseph Conrad when he arrived as a servant of the Société Anonyme Belge pour la Commerce du Haut Congo only fifty years before. During that voyage, even before he arrived at Boma and witnessed Belgium's criminal exploitation of the Congo, Conrad had begun to have doubts about the colonial project. 'Day after day the coastline was unchanging, as if the vessel were making no progress.' He regards the few settlements that they do pass as 'sordid' and 'dreary' and detects the ease with which one might go mad when, as far as the eye can see, there is 'nothing but ocean, sky, and the hair-thin green strip of bush vegetation' and he writes of a stationary warship, a 'ponderous vessel' that 'rose and fell on the slimy swell' and on whose mast the ensign hung limply. There is no sign of settlement on the shore but 'at regular intervals the long six-inch guns fired off shells into the unknown African continent, with neither purpose nor aim.'

I have read other accounts – for example, of the four Grangemouth children who were amongst the seavacs rescued from a torpedoed ship while being sent to Canada by the Children's Overseas Relocation Board. When interviewed, all four said they heard no explosion but received a warning by bell. The alarm came at 11.30 p.m. when the children were all in bed. They had, however, been warned to sleep in their clothes and so it was only a matter of finding their coats and shoes and making their way to the lifeboats. 'None of the children,' according to newspaper reports, 'showed any fear or feeling of nervousness.' When they arrived safely in port, they were handed a card with a tartanbound sprig of heather through it on which were printed these words:

'Warmest Congratulations.
We are all proud of your bravery.
Good luck.
From Mr Geoffrey Shakespeare,
Chairman, C.O.R.B.'

My father and his brothers did not come under the aegis of the Children's Overseas Relocation Board; theirs was a private enterprise, and in any case he had as his protector Eileen Nelson who was more scary and better resourced than any number of government agencies dedicated to the welfare of their citizens. I am sure that she would have agreed with the parents of these four children when interviewed by their local newspaper. They were adamant that evacuation was the best possible course for their children and they would sail again as soon as another boat became available. The children too were unanimous in their desire to go. When they did, they were each given a copy of the collected poems of Robert Burns, a souvenir of their native land for them to carry to their deaths or to Canada, whichever came first.

Fortunately, the brothers had no need of Mr Shakespeare's luck, although they did have the collected works of Robert Burns. Somewhere south of Luanda, Dad celebrates his fourteenth birthday. His brothers tease him for being old. A few days after that, an early-morning bell wakes them from their sleep – no doubt, the same bell that would have woken them had they been hit by a torpedo. They come on deck to be greeted by the sight of Table Bay in all its glory, a soft white cloth on Table Mountain and the city gleaming majestically below it. A voice on the tannoy says, 'Welcome to Cape Town.' For George – who has already told his mother that leaving home was 'the best day of his life' – this is the second best day. The sea is calm and sparkling and the city below the mountain seems to shine with promise.

Dad never spoke of this arrival, nor indeed of the departure, but many others have. Margaret Wood, another child evacuee sent out to South Africa three weeks earlier than my father, writes of the expectation that this would be only a short interlude. The war would be over 'by Christmas'. They would all be home soon. But at least they were well looked after. 'When we crossed the line (the equator) we had a big party, it was very riotous and ended by putting bread and jam down each others [sic] backs.'

The succeeding days are a whirl of meetings and press calls during which Robin and George, though not Dad, manage to get themselves photographed in Adderley Street with the Governor. Their picture appears in the following morning's papers. Fifty years later, Madge Wear, who was an escort for boys on a similar trip in 1940, recalled the thrill of these delights. 'Picking fruit off the trees was another forgotten luxury, and they all had bananas and oranges given to them – the first they had seen since 1939. My first memory was seeing Cape Town ablaze with lights at night – so strange after our blackout.' Dad and his brothers stay in dormitories on the property of the Governor's residence, which is then called Westbrook. 'You must be the Scots evacuees,' George remembers the Governor saying, 'Help yourself to some straw-berries.' Strawberries! Sun! Help yourself! Such luxury.

But it ends too soon. Nelly Bell collects them and puts them on a train to Grahamstown, where the Jesuit brothers of St Aidan's College are waiting to carry on where their mother has left off.

21. Second-generation bridge

'IT HAS BEEN estimated,' Rex Mackey writes, 'by an eminent authority, who had obviously nothing better to do, that the normal bridge session involves the average player in four hundred borderline decisions, one in three of which he will make incorrectly. This entails an incidence of 133.3 recurring critical strictures per partner per session, which is exactly the figure most conscientious workers in this field will arrive at, particularly in regard to the recurring part.'

He says this by way of introduction to the group of men who created the 'Acol' system of playing bridge. A decade after Harold Vanderbilt invented the game, and once Culbertson had successfully marketed it, huge confusion reigned in the actual playing of it. 'Bridge players of that era fell into two categories. They were either converts from Auction, or else had been taught Contract by players whose knowledge of the basic principles was sketchy. In either case their plight was an unhappy one.' Both Mackey and Alan Truscott catalogue many hands that would nowadays embarrass an average player but which were then bid and played by experts, Culbertson included. 'Further evidence is supplied by the spate of books inflicted on the defenceless public at this period, each advocating what its author euphemistically described as his "system".' Misunderstandings, both in social and tournament play, were rife. Howlers were commonplace. Disasters occurred both in declarer play and in the bidding, and the results were either horrifying or diverting, depending on whether 'one was the victim or the beneficiary'. This early incompetence may have had one inadvertent side-effect. Bridge became associated with the kind of repartee of which my father was particularly fond. When, at a major tournament, a competitor asked a kibitzer how he should have played a particular hand, for example, the reply was short and to the point, though not necessarily helpful: 'Under an assumed name.'

Something had to be done. Such was Culbertson's dominance in the United States that it is not surprising that innovation had to come from elsewhere. In England, 'the fundamentals of the game were even more imperfectly assimilated' than in the United States. But the popularity of the game was comparable. To that extent the 'invasion from the West' had triumphed. From its springboard in New York, bridge has become a game played all over the world. It spread quickly throughout Europe. The war would make it global as soldiers played it wherever they were sent.

But it was in London in 1938 and 1939 that a small group of men began to think seriously about the game and how it might be made better and more comprehensible. The best known and the acknowledged leader was Maurice Harrison-Gray, who had been a despatch rider during the First World War. He was 'tall, bald, mustachioed and impressive,' says Alan Truscott. Harrison-Gray, like Harold Vanderbilt, was a multi-talented man. As well as one of the leading bridge players and writers of his generation, he was also one of the country's leading lepidopterists.

Harrison-Gray met the second of the group at the Acol Club in London (named after the street in which the club had its premises). This was S.J. ('Skid') Simon.

They couldn't have been more different. One magazine at the time characterised them as Don Quixote and Sancho Panza. Where Harrison-Gray was tall, urbane and patrician, Simon was 'short, unkempt, with saturnine features, pulpy flesh and a shock of black hair above a loose, sensual mouth'. He spoke appalling English, and (in common with many Russians) never knowingly used the definite article. He had a similar aversion to pronouns.

John Clay recalls that a 'typical sentence would run: "Bid impeccable spade; butt in, two-H; partner, Free Cluck (three clubs). Pass.
Self, what? Self, free die (three diamonds)."'

And yet he wrote English beautifully. *Why You Lose at Bridge*,
which from 1946 onwards served as my father's bridge bible, was
voted in a recent survey of American Contract Bridge League
members the 'best bridge book ever', and is written in the clear-
est and most impeccable prose. The same applies to his columns
for *Punch* magazine and the twelve comic novels he co-authored
with Caryl Brahms.

Two other men were at this time playing at the Acol Club. One
was Iain MacLeod who was later lost to the game when he took up
a much less respectable career as a Member of Parliament and
Chancellor of the Exchequer. He was widely tipped to be a future
prime minister before his untimely death in 1970 at the age of
fifty-three. And there was Jack Marx, with whom Simon would
debate the essentials of what would become known as 'Acol' late
into the night. 'Simon may be described as the synthesist who
propounded the theories, and Marx as the analyst who broke them
down into their essential parts,' says Rex Mackey.

There was much to Acol that was technical, but what set it apart
from the theories that Culbertson and his generation proposed
was that it contained a better understanding of the nature of the

partnership. It was about 'a state of mind'. Skid Simon elaborated on this in various places. 'The Acol System,' he wrote, 'has often been described as an attitude of mind. It is never easy to explain an attitude, but I feel I must have a stab at explaining this one... The Acol attitude has realised that bidding is not an exact science, but a scientific estimation of mathematical probabilities. It has also realised that the probabilities to be estimated include the probable actions of opponents who regrettably happen to be present, and that the entire language for estimating is limited to thirty-eight bids and that that is not nearly enough to paint a complete picture of the hand most of the time or even part of the time.' And he iterates the view that MacLeod was to repeat some years later: 'There are two objectives in bridge. The first is to make the best of your cards, the second is to prevent the enemy making the best of theirs.'

Dad believed in Acol's famous dictum: 'Bid what you think you can make.' Don't think you have to be fancy for the sake of it. If you want to be in game, bid game. If you think a slam might be on, bid a slam. It shuts the opponents up and gets you where you want to be. Do it! And, when in doubt, bid one more, especially in a competitive auction where there is as much to be gained from keeping your opponents out of their best contract as there is to be got from being in yours.

In the United States, a new generation of experts was coming to contract bridge. Charles Goren first got into bridge because of a young woman who hosted a bridge party in Montreal in 1923. He later graduated in law and when he went home to Philadelphia, he bought Milton Work's *Auction Bridge* (the same volume that predicted auction bridge was embarking on an 'extended period of stability'). In 1936, Goren stopped practising law and turned his attention full-time to bridge. He moved from being Work's 'technical assistant', which meant that he wrote many of the columns that appeared worldwide under Work's byline, to having his own column. His writing was fresh and new and soon attracted followers. Then he published his first bridge book, *Winning Bridge Made Easy*. Initially, it was thought to have little chance of being a big seller because Culbertson's domination in bridge was complete. If it wasn't Culbertson, it wasn't bridge, went the thinking. But Goren had something more to offer, not least that his approach, like that of the Acol group in London, was blessed with a refreshing clarity and simplicity. In particular, he took Work's point count, which had hitherto been used mainly for valuing no trump hands, and extended it to all suit contracts. *Point Count Bidding at Contract Bridge* was priced at only $1 and quickly became a bestseller. It converted the American (and world) bridge public from Culbertson's 'honour tricks' to the point count. The book sold well and, on the day it was published, Goren gave up his law practice. Bridge and bridge writing were now earning him three or four times as much as he ever made from the law. And, as Culbertson's interest took him into politics, Goren soon became the dominant bridge writer. By the early 1940s, he had more columns in more newspapers than Culbertson.

But you make an impact in the bridge world not only by writing books, but also by winning tournaments. Goren formed a long-lasting and highly successful partnership with Helen Sobel. Together, they won virtually everything in sight and Goren soon found himself at the head of the American Contract Bridge League masterpoint table, a position he was to hold, uninterrupted, from 1944 until 1962. He was perfectly placed to cash in on the worldwide bridge boom that followed the end of the Second World War. *Contract Bridge Complete* and *New Contract Bridge Complete* won him followers all over the world and his name soon became synonymous with bridge, just as Culbertson's had been in the 1930s. He was sometimes called Mr Bridge and in 1958 even appeared on the cover of *Time* magazine. At the height of his fame, 34 million people were reading his weekly bridge column.

The Acol group had less success and less worldwide impact, but what was appealing about Goren was also appealing about their approach to the game: keep it simple. Make it easy for your partner and hard for your opponents.

In any case, they had to wait for the end of the war before they could gain international tournament success. While bridge in the United States continued pretty much as usual during the war, in Europe there was an obvious hiatus. Iain MacLeod had been on the verge of qualifying to represent Britain in the European championships of 1939 when a brief illness eliminated him from the selection process. It was several years before he played tournament bridge again, for he enlisted in the British Army as soon as the war began, and spent the next six years in uniform. There is a story, possibly apocryphal, that early on in the war an intelligence officer found a note which caused alarm. It read 'Ax, Kxxx, Qxxx, KQx', and the officer, who did not play bridge, immediately suspected a conspiracy. He approached MacLeod who 'immediately recognised it as a bridge hand he had scribbled down and thrown away – and not as a plot to overthrow the monarchy'. MacLeod was part of the Planning Staff for the D-Day invasions and was one of the men who landed in Normandy on D-Day itself. At the end of the war, 'the Acol group went into action. England won three straight European titles, with Harrison-Gray as the playing captain, the only successful playing captain in bridge history. Simon was his partner in 1948 and 1949, but an early death removed him from the scene.' He was replaced by Jack Marx in 1950. By this time, Iain MacLeod had been elected to Parliament as the Conservative member for the London constituency of Enfield. With bridge and politics making increasing demands on his time, something had to give. He became nonplaying captain of the British bridge team that went to the European Championships in Venice in 1951, but later that year was appointed to Churchill's cabinet when the Conservatives ousted Labour from office. MacLeod was the youngest man to hold the office of Minister of Health. He had to give up playing international bridge, although he still found time to publish his textbook, *Bridge is an Easy Game*. 'There's a copy in the library at Number 10 Downing Street,' John Clay writes, 'which bears MacLeod's inscription on the flyleaf: "This is the only book in this place that is certain to profit its reader".'

In *Bridge is an Easy Game*, MacLeod summarises the Acol approach to bidding:

> The Acol System has two main objectives:
> To make bidding easy for your partner
> To make bidding difficult for your opponent

The rest was detail. Bind your friends to you with hoops of steel; reject the rest.

Even while in government, MacLeod continued to play bridge, if not for his country then at least for money. Both in his bridge and in his politics, Iain MacLeod was a model for my father. MacLeod was only a few years older, but the gap was of the order of which heroes are formed. Terence Reese wrote of him that his outstanding characteristic was 'a dynamic aggression. He is always on the attack. Of all the players I have ever known he most exactly mirrors his character in his bridge – in both there is a pugnacity that seems reckless but which is, in fact, founded upon a profound knowledge – sometimes self-knowledge – and justified self-confidence.'

22. A brief war

WHAT STRIKES ME now as curious about Dad is that he only
ever found that self-belief at the bridge table. Away from it, he
shrank, not completely but noticeably. At the table – his precious
'square yard of freedom' – the certainties he experienced matched
the certainties he expected. Away from it, this was anything but
the case. Away from the table, life is fractured, unpredictable,
various. He is not in control. Greater and darker forces have
severed him from his family and tossed him adrift on a turbu-
lent sea. And, even though he bobs successfully on the unstable
waters, he begins to hate the absence of control.

Still, at least he is 'good' at school. His parents, he is sure, will be
pleased. From an early age, they have drummed into him the
importance of 'excellence'. It becomes a catchphrase of theirs and

later of his, and one he is apt in later life to aim at his children. 'Make with the excellence,' he says, in such a way that we genuinely believe it doesn't matter much at what – as long as it is something.

At the end of 1943, he leaves school (in South Africa the school year and the calendar year coincide) having matriculated with distinction. He is top of his class and the top student in the Cape Province. He wins a scholarship to the University of the Witwatersrand where he has decided to study Chemical Engineering. He is not sad to leave school. He says goodbye to his brothers and moves to Johannesburg where he takes a room in one of the student residences. The big city delights him; there are libraries and dances, bridge clubs and music. There are women, with whom he has always been shy, but who are often quick to fall for his sly humour – he is a master of the semi-ironic aside – and his elegant, if leggy, dancing. And they like the fact that whatever subject they're studying seems easy to him, for he is exceptionally bright. He plays bridge with friends. He doesn't neglect his studies, nor does he take them too seriously. He is young, but he is tall and good-looking and these are times when cities like Johannesburg are wide open for young men with initiative and ideas, brains and confidence.

And yet university is a disappointment. For all the social whirl of Johannesburg in wartime, he still feels terribly alone. George is still at St Aidan's. Robin, the nearest he has to a peer, is mildly asthmatic and has been sent to a different school near Pietersburg in the Highveld. Dad hasn't seen his parents since 1940. The letters home are a chore. The letters from home feel like a litany of complaint. And he is short of money; a scholarship will only take him so far.

He also, I suspect, feels he has yet to prove himself. He has not yet fully made the transition from being a boy to being a man. In the absence of a father, he will have to find his own rite of passage. There are girlfriends, of course, but that is not quite what he has in mind. And there is politics – but he has never been that interested in politics. Rather, he has – despite the great rift – taken from his parents a narrow conservative politics. He believes in family. He is instinctively a libertarian, but he craves law and order. Later in life, he will approve of Mrs Thatcher, while despising her strident tones and her relish for the fight. He despises tardiness and sloth; he distrusts the masses. He might quote Auden – but only selectively.

> And always the loud angry crowd
> Very angry and very loud
> Law Is We,
> And always the soft idiot softly Me.

He prefers the soft idiot to the loud and angry crowd, but he wants more than anything to belong – to anyone, to anything – and perhaps it is with this in mind that in January 1945 he makes his way to a recruiting office and enlists in the South African Army. He becomes an artilleryman in the Sixth South African Armoured Brigade. By March, he is in North Africa; by April, he is part of the Allied forces, mopping up resistance in the valleys of northern Italy. He spends his days some distance behind the lines, as he (I suspect disingenuously) puts it, 'lobbing shells at people I never saw' and playing bridge. He learns to smoke a pipe, a habit which will stay with him until he dies, a habit, indeed, which may be said to have killed him. The familiar towns are captured and subdued, one by one. Monte Sole, Bologna, Padua, Milan.

I remember, some years later, I told him about a trip a friend and I made in the Apennines when we made our way on foot and over the course of several days from Bologna to Lucca and then on to Florence. Somewhere on the baby slopes of Monte Cimone, we came across a farmer beside a pockmarked wall, and got into conversation. This was 1990, some forty-five years after the events in question, but the farmer described in astonishing detail how as a young boy he had hidden and watched as German troops shot his father, his uncle and two brothers against the wall which, even now, he preserved in their memory. As he spoke, he traced the contours of the wall with his hand, and his fingers found their way from one hole to the next as they must have done many, many times over the intervening years. I remember also how Dad's eyes clouded when I told him this story, and how he let his head fall forward and sat there very still, and for several minutes thereafter said nothing at all.

When, finally, he emerged from the reverie into which my story had plunged him, it was to ask only whether we'd enjoyed the walk, which was his version, as I well knew, of doubling for takeout, which I did by moving the conversation on to other records I have read of soldiers playing bridge.

In Kansas, officers of the 39th Bomb Group of the US Airforce recall that they spent several months 'on a state of constant alert (mostly playing bridge)', which reminds me of the suburb of the northern English town of Bradford known as Idle where it is poss- ible even now to visit the 'Idle Working Men's Club'.

Bridge is not only popular with the enlisted men but also with their commanders. All through the war General Dwight D. Eisenhower continued to indulge his passion for the game. 'On November 7, 1942, he relaxed at the card table while waiting for news of the landing at Casablanca in North Africa. One of the other players was General Alfred Guenther, last heard of directing the Culbertson-Lenz match in 1930.' Guenther and Eisenhower were, in fact, bridge friends for many years. After the war, the former Supreme Commander, Allied Forces in Europe – under whose command my father eventually fell – took it easy for a while as President of Columbia University. The post suited him because it left his afternoons free for playing bridge. Truscott takes up the story: 'One day he was at the card table and was told by a club servant that he was wanted on the telephone. He was not at all pleased at being disturbed and grumbled off.' He returned with a thunderous expression on his face, and his partner, a young player called Caulkins, asked what the matter was.

The 'matter' was President Truman who had called to ask Eisenhower to take up the appointment as head of NATO in Paris.

Truscott reports the conversation:

> 'Will you go?'
>
> With a shrug, 'If the president says go, you go.'
>
> 'Who will you take as your number two?'
>
> 'Well, I ought to take Bedell Smith. But I think I'll take Guenther because he's a better bridge player.'
>
> Which is how General Alfred Maximilian Guenther subsequently became head of NATO when Eisenhower returned to the United States to run for the presidency.

Eisenhower was not the only world leader obsessed with the game. The view of Hilaire Belloc reflects the extraordinary appeal of the game for men and women, and for all classes and political persuasions, for it is a curiosity of bridge that, although its roots are among the leisured classes, it has found as many adherents on the left as on the right.

> The accursed Power which stands on Privilege
> (And Goes with Women, and Champagne and Bridge)
> Broke – and Democracy resumed her reign;
> (Which goes with Bridge and Women and Champagne).

Bridge in China, for example, has its roots in the cafés of Paris in the 1920s, where it was part of the mix of ideas and revolutionary fervour enjoyed by middle-class students and taken back to China on their return. Deng Xiaoping worked for a time at the Renault factory in Paris and learned the game while staying at the apartment of Zhou Enlai. He remained a fanatical player for the rest of his life, even in defiance of the orders of Chairman Mao, who regarded bridge as a middle-class affectation. Mao banned the game in 1949 and it remained an illegal activity in China for the next thirty years. But, even through a period of internal exile during the Cultural Revolution, Deng continued to play the game. He is reputed to have been a 'crafty' and 'political' player, basing his success as much on his estimation of the weaknesses of his opponents as on the strength of his own cards. Throughout his time in power, Deng played bridge three or four times a week and by all accounts was a world-class player, 'as good as Omar Sharif', according to Kathy Wei-Sender, who is herself world-class. Bridge became legal in 1979, and the game is now played at every level. There are more bridge players in China than in any other country in the world. Because of his promotion of the game, Deng was honoured at the 1981 World Championships when he was voted, by the International Bridge Press Association, Bridge Personality of the Year, a unique honour for a world leader. With his support, China joined the World Bridge Federation and in 1995 went on to host the World Championships.

Deng resigned all offices some years before he died – although he remained paramount in China – and at the time of his death his only official title was that of honorary president of the Chinese Bridge Federation. Of course, his motivation for keeping his love of the game in the public eye remained at least partly political. He is often quoted as saying, 'When people see me swimming, they think I am physically fit. And when they hear of me playing bridge, they think I am mentally fit.'

And it is not just China. The war takes bridge around the world. From the prison camps of Burma to the parade grounds of Calcutta, people are playing bridge. It will be some years before countries other than 'old' Europe and 'new' America start producing world champions – but that time will come. By the end of the war, bridge is played by more people in more countries than ever before. The war has made it a global game.

Dad sees out the balance of hostilities in Italy, 'playing bridge in a state of constant alert', but some distance behind 'the action'. His unit is in Milan on 28 April 1945 when Mussolini and his lover are hung out to dry in the Piazzale Loreto. 'God, what an ignoble end,' Eisenhower says, with elegant understatement.

For some months after the war ends, troops hang around Europe waiting to be sent 'home'. My father is in due course demobbed. But he is not sent home. His nationality is by now disputed. When he left Scotland for South Africa, he had no passport, only a name tag and an address. When he enlisted into the South African Army, he was given a South African passport. And this document determined where the army would send him. And so he sails, together with the rest of his unit, back to Cape Town. He arrives there towards the end of 1945 and makes his way back to Johannesburg. A place has been kept for him at the University of the Witwatersrand and he now has a little money, which when coupled with a bursary or two and an ex-serviceman's grant enables him to resume his studies amidst the social whirl of Johannesburg.

He is now an ex-serviceman, a soldier. He smokes, he drinks. He has looked into the abyss and survived. In that sense at least, he has had 'a good war'. His parents are not forgotten exactly, but nor are they part of his life. The rift that opened when his metal trunk first appeared in the sitting room in Greenbank Road in the late summer of 1940 has become an unbridgeable chasm. It will be another four years before he sees Rose and Tom again. When, finally, he does arrive in Edinburgh in the autumn of 1949 his youngest brother – my uncle Brian – looks at him quizzically. 'Who are you?' he wants to know. And what the bloody hell are you doing here? Robin and George returned home at the end of the war, young enough still to complete their schooling at the Holy Cross School. For them, the South African adventure was an interlude. For Dad, it was everything. And, after the freedom and light of Johannesburg, Scotland does not feel much like a place to come home to. It feels like a place he left. He stays for less than a year. His future lies elsewhere.

◆

PART IV

A VALEDICTION FORBIDDING MOURNING

23. The far side

SOME JOURNEYS IT is better not to travel alone. In the months after Dad's death, my brother and I see more of each other than usual. There is the trip to the Drakensberg where I teach the kids how to play bridge while David shows them how to tie knots. Another time, we go to Tanzania where we and my elder daughter attempt to climb Mount Kilimanjaro. Even after all this time, David's still angry with Dad, fuming in fact. One night, looking out across the African plains, he tells me about the time he found Dad having a nightcap. Mum and Jackie were in Europe; I was at boarding school. It was just David and Dad. David took the bottle of whisky and poured it down the drain. There was a tense stand-off before David turned and walked out.

'I never really felt we spoke again,' he says.

And, in the autumn of 2004, he and I head for Siberia, together with Cal and a friend who lives and works in Moscow. 'You'll like the silences,' my friend says. 'Nowhere has silences like Siberia.' It was, we agreed, both a promise and a threat. 'I like to listen to the wind,' he adds. He is a scholar of some distinction, known in his field for his formidable intellect, his carefully phrased arguments and the intimidating reach of his knowledge. The idea of him listening to the wind has a certain quixotic appeal. As, indeed, does the idea of him liking Siberia. He had, after all, spent a large portion of his childhood there when Stalin imprisoned his parents.

In addition to a promise and a threat, it is a curious 'sell'. We are going to the wilds of Kamchatka in the Russian Far East. The peninsula is famous for many things – for its volcanoes and bears, for the streams filled with salmon and for Avachinsky Bay filled with the rusting hulks of the Soviet Pacific Fleet. It was the promise of bears and salmon that caught Cal's attention but I harboured a sneaking interest in the tarnished fleet.

Kamchatka is known too as the place from which the Danish explorer Vitus Bering, then in the service of the Russian imperial court, launched his successful, but fatal, second attempt to prove that America and Asia were not in fact joined. And it was while working for Bering that the botanist Stepan Krasheninnikov wrote his astonishingly accurate portrait of the undisturbed lands and people of Kamchatka. The work was published first in 1755 and remains in print to this day. He, like all travellers to Kamchatka, was impressed by its size and its distances, and by its relentless, inhospitable beauty.

And, as we talked about it in the rushing traffic of central Moscow, the idea appealed more and more. Within minutes of plunging into the rude cacophony of Sheremetevo airport's domestic departure hall, I found myself longing for silence. Any silence. Kamchatka's would have done nicely.

Kamchatka, however, was still 4,000 miles away. On his first trip it took Bering four years to get there and back. The peninsula is nine hours and 120 degrees of longitude ahead of Moscow, twelve hours ahead of London. You don't need to reset your watch, for night is day and day is night. As we flew I traced our route on the map: north past the ghastly Soviet labour camps of Vorkuta before crossing the Urals and heading east over the endless tundra.

We take off in the afternoon, but soon plunge into the night. David watches a late moon rising at 15 degrees an hour before we find ourselves flying into a sunrise that appears unwilling ever quite to happen. It's his first visit to Russia. He counts the three great Siberian rivers – the Ob, the Yenisei and the Lena. One by one they mark the passing hours.

We are staying in Nalychevo, one of five 'nature parks' run by the provincial government of Kamchatka *Oblast*. It extends for some 300,000 hectares and is dominated by three volcanoes – Avachinsky, Koriaksky and A'ag, which separate it from Petropavlovsk, seventy kilometres to the south. Our helicopter lands in a soft, wide valley, a basin almost, filled with birch trees and blueberry bushes, rivers and hot springs. There are no fences to these parks. The wildlife – bears, wolves, wolverines, Arctic foxes and small rodents – come and go. Five species of salmon come to Nalychevo to spawn, but the rivers also have plenty of smaller, more feisty fish. And the valley is surrounded by towering snow-covered peaks, mountains forged in violence and now silent, remote and beautiful.

But not inactive. We listen for rumblings in the earth. I expect them to start any moment, to send billowing clouds into the night sky. From the helicopter, the volcanoes seemed small, conquered. From their foothills, they seem to glower against the darkness, daring those who would to remain within reach. We can picture the fury of an eruption. We can imagine the way the red lava would have flowed across the mountain's icy, alabaster skin.

People in such a place are self-selecting. They come there not by chance but because they too value the peace and quiet, the relationship to nature which is neither hostile nor subjugated. In our immediate circle, there was Irina, the cook, and Volodya, the guide. And then there was Yuri, one hand damaged in an industrial accident, who teaches Cal rope tricks and gives him a gorilla mask with which to terrorise us all over the coming days. There are also the guards who work for the park, and a smattering of volunteers – pensioners, sailors on shore leave and students on vacation. All of them give up their summers to work in the park, unpaid. One evening after dinner, there is a singsong at which a succession of Russians sing mocking songs of love or the motherland.

One of the singers is Waldemar, a thin freckled man with a sailor's beard and a command of his audience. 'I am from Belarus,' he says, as though that explains everything. Waldemar is something of a nationalist, although his story is very Russian. 'I cannot go home,' he says in response to another question. 'I have been in Russia ten years, but I am poor. I can't go home. My parents will say, "Ten years you have been away! Ten years in Russia! Where is the money?" To go home I must have money.'

I like Waldemar. He brings us rhododendron stems ('good for the liver') and wild spring onions ('Delicious, like garlic. You try?') and it is he who catches the 25-pound salmon on which we feed for two days.

Cal, David and I do what boys do. We fish in the rivers, bathe in the hot springs and swing from the birch trees. One could do worse, said Robert Frost, 'than be a swinger of birches'. For the child and the man, it is good in both the going and the coming back. One night under the wide sky, when there is no light but starlight, and no sounds but the breeze on bark and the occasional rustle of a mouse in the blueberry meadow, we take a midnight 'banya', and beat each other with birch twigs before letting the hot steam leach away our city cares.

When it rains, we play a form of three-handed whist. Although he is of the same generation as Dad, our companion does not play bridge. In his extraordinary life – from the Jewish quarters of Vilnius to the prison camps of the Altai, from his soldiering days on Burma Road in Palestine to professorships in Manchester and Moscow – he has managed to avoid the reach of Culbertson's game.

'Strange but true,' he says.

Later that year, I return to Moscow on other business. One evening, my companion and I take the opportunity to visit Moscow's only bridge club. I have arranged to meet and interview Tatiana Ponomareva, a member of the Russian women's team that won the gold medal at the 2004 Bridge Olympiad. It is the country's first medal in international bridge. It may well be a sign of things to come. In the open contest, the Russian men's team won the bronze medal, coming third to Holland and the seemingly unbeatable Italian team.

Tatiana is as surprised by their victory as anyone.

'I started playing in 1990,' she tells me. She speaks mostly in English but every now and then she has to grope for the correct phrase. From time to time, my friend acts as translator.

'It was a strange time in Russia. The Soviet time had ended, and a new time had started. But we do not know what this new time is. We do not know what it means.'

She has just graduated with a Master's degree in Mathematics from Moscow University, but she was not sure that there was any future for her in Russia.

'Nowadays people can go straight into business,' she says. And so she and a group of friends decided to wait and see. There were some friends who had started to play bridge, which she took to be a sign of the times. Since the Brezhnev era, bridge had been more or less forbidden in Russia. Certainly, no bridge clubs were allowed. But now things were opening up and – like so many great bridge players before her – she started playing to gain the attention of a friend of a friend. The friend of a friend is now her husband.

Tatiana looks too ordinary to be a world champion. She is a tall woman with straight hair and easy, soft features. She smiles quietly, as I remind her of moments along the way to her victory – as if she needs reminding. Every minute is etched in her memory. But she is not too carried away by her victory.

'You don't win tournaments by always bidding the right contract,' she says. 'Sometimes you take chances. Sometimes they
work.'

The Russians' final margin of victory in the Olympiad was
twelve international match points (IMPs are a mechanism for cal-
culating advantage in duplicate bridge). And they picked up
seventeen IMPs on a single hand (known in tournament bridge
as a 'board') when Tatiana's partner, Victoria Gromova, made a
diffi-cult small slam in hearts. Other pairings playing with the
same cards managed to go at least two down in the same contract
and some went down in a contract of 4 ♥. It seems the Americans
made a poor play. In a key moment, Tobi Sokolow, one of the
game's great players and a very experienced tournament competitor, failed to 'give count' for her trump holding; as a result,
her partner did not lead a club, which Sokolow would have been
able to trump and so to defeat the contract. The Russians made
6 ♥, worth 1,430 points. In duplicate bridge, each team has two
pairs, playing in separate rooms. In one room, Team A sits 'North-
South'. In the other room. Team B sits in that position. That way,
players from each team play with exactly the same cards. The
question is not what you 'make', but whether what you make – or
what you prevent your opponents from making – scores better
than what your opponents make with the same cards. In Istanbul,

the Americans in the other room played in the same contract, but went two down, which was worth another 200 points to the Russians. Altogether a difference of 1,630 points, or seventeen IMPs – more than the final margin of victory. On such decisions are championships won and lost.

I was in Istanbul for the Olympiad and watched the final between Russia and America on the vugraph (a projection system whereby the play is relayed on to a screen for a large audience) in the main theatre at the conference centre where the tournament took place. The audience's sympathy was almost universally with the underdogs – bridge is that kind of game – and in this case the underdogs were the Russians. The final took place over two days. Going into the final session, the Russians held a lead of thirty-five IMPs. But the Americans started strongly. In the first five boards, they gained a total of twenty-three IMPs. The margin was down to only twelve IMPs when board twenty-two came up on the vugraph. The audience watched as the play began. Would the Russians bid the slam? Would they make it? In the other room, Randi Montin of the USA bid to a small slam, but made only ten tricks. The audience knew this hand could secure victory for the Russians. The experts didn't think it could be made. 'With a club lead, I don't think there is a chance,' said Michael Rosenberg, who was commentating on vugraph at the time. In the open final being played, Norberto Bocchi, one of the Italian world champions, went down in 4 ♥ with the same cards. A club was duly led and these were the cards:

NORTH

Molson

♠ K 9 5
♥ 5 2
♦ 10 8 6
♣ K 7 5 4 2

WEST

Ponomareva

♠ A 10 6 3 2
♥ K Q 7
♦ 4
♣ Q J 10 6

EAST

Gromova

♠ Q 7
♥ A J 8 6 3
♦ A 9 7
♣ A 9 8

SOUTH

Sokolow

♠ J 8 4
♥ 10 9 4
♦ K Q J 5 3 2
♣ 3

Victoria Gromova won the club lead and then played two rounds of trumps. She had to keep one in dummy. The key play came when she attempted to finesse spades; this failed and North won with her king. She was now on lead. Had she led a club, South would have trumped it and the contract would have failed. But she didn't. For whatever reason – most commentators assumed that she thought South had started with only two trumps – North led a diamond. East won with the ace and the contract was secure. 'A big result for Russia,' said one commentator with elegant understatement.

The vugraph audience was very knowledgeable. They gasped and then cheered when the diamond lead came down. It looked like the underdogs would win – and indeed they did. The Americans made further gains in the remaining ten hands – but not enough to win.

'In tournaments, you sometimes win points by playing badly,' Tatiana says. 'And sometimes you do it by playing well. We did some of both.' She knows they were lucky to win, but she is glad to have 'put Russia on the map'. She is pleased that her country is now part of the world of bridge.

A few weeks earlier in Kamchatka, a misty depression has set in. Heavy cloud squats on the surrounding volcanoes. The helicopters will be unable to fly; we are advised to prepare ourselves to spend a few more days in Nalychevo.

'Cool,' says Cal to my friend. 'You can learn bridge.' My friend, the professor from Moscow, who is sixty-five years older than Cal, looks only slightly surprised to be taking lessons from a nine-year-old. Cal doesn't care. He has the cards out before we even sit down.

I start out on the basics, but I am hardly into my spiel before he takes over.

'What you have to understand is that the idea of the game is first to reach a "contract" by agreeing how many "tricks" you and your partner will make. And then you need to try to make them. A trick is a round of four cards, right? Each player plays one card. There are fifty-two cards in the pack and there are therefore thirteen tricks to be won. Got that? Fifty-two divided by four is thirteen...'

David and I look at each other.

'Oh, dear God,' he says. 'Where have I heard this before?' But really he's remembering those evenings at home when we were young and the evenings later when Dad lay dying. After our game, Cal and I find him by the river, listening to the wind in the blueberry meadows.

There is nothing, our friend said, to compare with the silences of Siberia.

24. The squeeze

FOR ME IT was a time of airports and rental cars. I remember one particular flight I made to London while Dad lay in hospital.

We take off as normal from Johannesburg International, heading north and across Africa. But perhaps an hour after take-off, with Harare somewhere off to the right, the captain comes on the intercom system. There is, he says, a fault with one of the engines. He has had to shut it down. With that insouciant, prac-tised captain's drawl, he says it is fortunate that the aircraft has three more. In his opinion, it is perfectly possible to fly to London with only three engines but, on balance, he thinks it better if we turn around and make our way back to Johannesburg where the problem can be checked and, if necessary, rectified. So we turn around and fly for another hour back to Johannesburg. The cabin staff serve us meals that no one eats. Just short of Johannesburg, the pilot speaks to us again. The fuel tanks are too full to attempt a landing. We must first jettison fuel. With this in mind, we will circle for some time while we offload the gasoline. We should not be alarmed to see it pouring from the wings of the aircraft, and even as he speaks a silver line seems to be drawn by an invisible hand from the wings and to plunge into the darkness below. It will not reach the ground. The fuel vaporises almost immediately and disappears to who knows where, and all that is left is a thin gossamer line stretching out into the night sky like the ashes of the dead, while the cabin lights are dimmed.

I think about Dad and bridge, bridge and Dad. The game, as he knew too well, allows for the most exquisite cruelty and aggression as well as moments of extreme beauty. It reached its peak in the 1930s, when Dad was young. It soon achieved a 'status as something people aspired to, had its own social cachet, and the ability to play the game became one of the key social attributes'. Before 1929, before Culbertson and the Great Depression, bridge had been a game for the affluent classes. The Depression changed this. Bridge eclipsed hitherto more popular games like pinochle and poker. Mrs Grace Lapham, who was head of the Child Training Institute in London at the time, records that more than 20 per cent of requests for governesses specified that they should play bridge. As one parent put it, 'By respecting his bids, you teach him to respect yours and a child who gets intelligent and interesting answers to his bridge questions will be more likely to come to his parents with his more important questions.'

In my parents' house, these questions were as likely to be answered in the form of a metaphor, which, as often as not, was couched in the language of bridge. The certainties of the 'square yard of freedom' were infinitely preferable to (and more comprehensible than) the noisy stirrings of African nationalism outside the door. So it was that, while Soweto burned, we played bridge. John Clay identifies why this might have seemed attractive. 'Bridge requires players to do the right thing, hence much of its middle-class appeal to the rule-conscious and convention-minded.' But the 'right thing' is a slippery beast and I suspect that for my father – as for the great players of the game – the rules were there to be broken. 'Rules are made for the obedience of fools,' he often quoted, 'and the guidance of wise men,' and we understood that he counted himself amongst the latter, in fact, as their finest representative. And, thinking about it now, I realise that the saying came not from something he had read but from his father, who no doubt muttered it by way of explanation and excuse (as my father did), as he reached for one drink too many, or as he made an unusual, unexplained, work-it-out-for-yourself bid or discarded an ace in order to create an entry to dummy.

'Another level of the appeal was the depth and complexity of the game,' John Clay says. 'It provided intellectual stimulus in addition to its social function. Educated, literate people welcomed this complexity, while for those lower down the social ladder it could become a vehicle for self-improvement and social advancement.' I have no doubt that this is largely true. My grandparents liked the game because it was cheap, accessible and intellectually stimulating. It appealed to their solid middle-class aspirations. It was undoubtedly 'good'. My father liked it because it gave him a platform on which to show off his quick thinking, his mathematical prowess and his imagination. My grandmother liked it because it made them *better* people. And both of them liked it as a rich source of metaphor, which they could harvest at will in their conversations with their children.

'You must let them know who's boss,' my father would repeat as he dealt the cards. 'They' in this context would have been my mother and sister seated beside us at the table, but, within the confines of the game, 'they' were as foreign and threatening as any number of African nationalists marching through the streets of Durban. 'Never let them forget who you are.'

This question, one he returned to often, is biblical and is, for example, what the Pharisees asked John the Baptist, suspecting him of purporting to be the Messiah. John, rather than answer directly the question of 'Who are you?', preferred to be oblique. 'I am not the Christ,' he replied, which satisfied his inquisitors and begged another answer to the central question of identity. The very same question – 'Tu Quis Es?' – was also the text chosen by Bishop Hugh Latimer when, in 1529, he composed and preached his famous 'sermons on the cards'. That the sermons were preserved until now owes as much to Latimer's subsequent martyrdom at the hands of Bloody Mary as it does to their theological or philosophical insights, but they are of interest to us because they contain the first recorded use of trumps as a metaphor – in this case for the Holy Spirit and His works.

Latimer was by all accounts a strange young man. We don't know exactly when he was born, although it is thought to have been in or around 1491. He appears at times to have been introverted and wilful, moody and withdrawn. But clearly he had a brilliant mind. He surfaces in the written records when he wins a scholarship to study at Clare College, Cambridge. The records are patchy regarding his academic career, but he acquired a Master's degree at the age of about twenty-four, and was ordained as a priest in the Catholic Church six years later. He went on to take a further degree in Divinity, at which time he argued publicly against those like Melancthon, who had begun to dismiss the Pope and his 'coterie' as amoral and corrupt.

By the beginning of the sixteenth century, various card games were growing in popularity in England, particularly early forms of whist. At Cambridge, the practice became so widespread that the authorities felt it necessary to control and limit the time people played cards. They disapproved of the game, and the early statutes of St John's College forbade the use of cards or dice except around Christmastime when a limited amount of playing – or gambling – was permitted.

Ever the bright young preacher, anxious to make a name for himself, Latimer proceeded to work this up into an overwrought – but strangely memorable – sermon. 'And whereas you are wont to celebrate Christmas in playing at cards, I intend, by God's grace, to deal unto you Christ's cards, wherein ye shall perceive Christ's rule. The game that we shall play shall be called the triumph, which, if it be played well, he that dealeth shall win; the layers shall likewise win; and the standers and lookers upon shall do the same; insofar as there is no man that is willing to play at this triumph with these cards, but they shall all be winners and no losers.'

'Not at my table, they won't,' said my father. The task was to make sure that he – and by extension I – was a winner and not a loser.

Latimer's sermon had at least one desired effect. It brought him to the attention of Henry VIII, and the following year he was called to preach before the King at Windsor. A chaplaincy in Wiltshire soon followed, but these were unpredictable times and, in the following years, Latimer veered between Royal and Diocesan favour and the Tower. When Cranmer became Archbishop of Canterbury, Latimer was restored to his post in the Church and was known to have preached before the King on all the Wednesdays of Lent in 1535. He became Bishop of Worcester the same year, but resigned in protest at the King's final break with Rome and the so-called Act for Abolishing Diversity of Opinion. But Henry died and Latimer was restored to his post during the relatively trouble-free reign of Edward VI. The restoration of a Catholic monarch in the form of Queen Mary, however, proved his undoing. Called to account for his 'protestant' beliefs, Latimer, along with Thomas Cranmer and Nicholas Ridley, was unable to express any faith in transubstantiation and was duly condemned to be burned at the stake, even though then and now it was and is widely agreed that their true crime was to have conspired with Henry against Catherine of Aragon.

On 16 October 1555, they were burned to death. Latimer's last words were: 'Be of good comfort, Master Ridley, and play the man; we shall this day, by God's grace, light such a candle in England as I trust shall never be put out.' What fascinates me most is not his courage to the end, nor his sermons on the cards, but the story of his brother of whom we know little except that, in an act of infinitely tender violence, he brought bags of gunpowder to the execution and draped them about Latimer's neck. And, when asked why, he said that there was little he could do to help the condemned man. His only desire was to speed his brother's departure and so to reduce his suffering. In this, at least, he was successful for, while Cranmer and Ridley suffered long in the flames, Latimer, in a dramatic and enviable death, burned, fizzed and was gone. It was with a certain morbid interest that I noted the details of his passing. The 'bill of charges' for the immolation of Ridley and Latimer amounted to 25 shillings and 2 pence, of which fully 50 per cent was for the 'three loads of wood faggots' and only 2 shillings and 8 pence went to pay the four labourers who built the pyre and fastened the chains.

25. Coming and going

THERE IS NO gunpowder to speed Dad's passing. After Christmas, he is admitted to hospital. He has difficulty eating because of a cancerous obstruction in his throat. He starts to lose weight fast.

David calls me at my office in London. 'You'd better come,' he says. 'Tonight would be good. They operate tomorrow.'

'Tomorrow?'

'*Ja*. The doctor reckons it's fifty–fifty.'

'I'm on my way. Have you called Jackie?'

'She's coming.'

'How's Mum?'

But neither of us is ever quite sure how Mum is and the question goes unanswered. How do we expect her to be? They've been married for nearly fifty years.

I go home to pack and to say goodbye to my girlfriend and our children. My suitcase looks like something a funeral director takes on holiday: dark suit, white shirt, dark tie, black shoes ... two pairs of swimming trunks, sandals, a couple of faded T-shirts, two or three baseball caps. On the flight, sleep is impossible. I stare for hours out the dark window until I see the first traces of a red dawn lighten the sky above Mozambique. It feels strange to be sealed in this silent cocoon in the sky. I try to imagine Dad.

'He's thin,' David has warned me. 'I mean, *really* thin.'

'He always was,' I say.

'Not like this.'

I am uncomfortably aware that I might be too late. Perhaps he has lost consciousness. Perhaps he is already dead.

I shake my head. Too many memories. Too much to take in, but I cannot help trying to assemble something from the jumble of images that course through my mind. How I see Dad is a different question. Even now, two years after he died, I find that I have difficulty stopping the speeding carousel of images in my mind. If, briefly, I do succeed in freezing the frame, I catch him seated at the bridge table in the sitting room, thirteen cards fanned in one hand.

His pipe is in his mouth, probably unlit. His unruly white hair – it has been white for as long as I can remember, although once it must have been dark – falls forward over his crevassed brow. His forelock is, in fact, not wholly white, but off-yellow, the effect of years of nicotine making its way past his eyes. His face is unnaturally long, a vast acreage of forehead plummeting down to pleasant and even features. It is jagged and craggy, covered with lines, scars and wrinkles. There are no straight lines. It reminds me of a waterfall in the dry season, the washed rocks bleaching in the unaccustomed sun. His nose is big and even, his lips full and sensitive. He wears a small moustache and has what are sometimes described as thoughtful eyes. They are deep set, grey and steady. They have a watery quality too; except when he is grinning, he looks like a man on the verge of tears. His legs are crossed, right over left, and, like his forehead, they are longer than one would reasonably have thought possible, so much so that he may from time to time cross them twice and tuck his right foot behind his left calf. He is wearing short trousers and a checked shirt and he peers from beneath shaggy brows at me or his cards or the monkeys that used to come to steal fruit from the garden.

He is smiling as he waits for play to begin, but softly and to himself, at some unspoken thought. He was not one to reminisce, at least not publicly, though it was possible from time to time, should I be particularly bloody-minded and should the weather have cooled a little, to get him to acknowledge that the past existed and that it might not be without interest to stroll a little down memory lane. But his memory lane is not the wisteria-lined avenue that the name suggests, but something altogether more noisy and disruptive, a place to be visited at one's peril, a road full of dead ends and wrong turnings, sudden yawning chasms and unexpected rock falls, and peopled by gangsters, vagabonds and (worse) fools. And, while peril may have been something that appealed to him in theory, he lived too long and too well not to know that, before heading into danger, one must first secure one's exits.

And, besides, his experience of life was of a dangerous and lawless place where charlatans prosper. Neal Ascherson puts it neatly when describing their native Scotland: 'But there are those countries,' he writes, 'which have left the past in its original condition: a huge, reeking tip of unsorted rubbish across which scavengers wander, pulling up interesting fragments which might fetch a price or come in handy. Scotland has been one of these.'

It is true of Dad, too, for the little he spoke of his past comes to me now as shards of glass that may as easily draw blood as catch the light. As I wander through the curious landfill of my memories, I struggle to bring order to the chaotic and tumbling fragments, part fact, part myth, the unsorted stuff of a life lived more or less across the twentieth century. And sometimes the broken glass seems more like water, mercurial and mobile, plunging over cataracts, disappearing into deep wells, slipping through my fingers into a parched desert. Even in its liquid form, it catches the light and twists it this way and that and the light is at once turbid and bright. And, at other times still, it comes to me as a chorus of glittering melancholy of the sort one might hear carried faintly from the distance on the night air, the silent reproachful stars withdrawing into the softening clouds that creep in from the west.

I can hear Dad laughing now except that, when Dad laughed, you didn't so much hear him as see him and – if you were in a car, say – *feel* him. His laugh could make a car shake until it squeaked. In the back seat, we children would nudge each other while Dad's shoulders heaved up and down. The cars – the whole succession of cars that populated our childhood, the Peugeots and the Fiats, the Mercedes and the Nissans – would bounce with him and we bounced too. Nowadays, when my children want to tease me, they mimic the rise and fall of his shoulders.

'You laugh like Tom,' says my daughter. 'Just don't dress like him, OK?' My daughter is fourteen, an age when fashion matters. When she says she doesn't want me to dress like Tom, she means that I shouldn't wear short trousers and yellow cardigans, long socks and *veldskoen*.

'It's how he was,' I say by way of explanation. As a child and as an adult, he wore shorts in all weathers, in the cold and the moist and the heat of summer too. Roaming the 'Braids', the fields south of Edinburgh, he came to love the elements, the way the fronts would sweep across Scotland from the west.

He loved the weather reports and their relentless repetitions. Time and again, fronts, hot and cold, warm and wet, form over the Atlantic and wash across this island, always the same pattern repeated. It is an industry in itself for the forecasters and the recorders, the broadcasters and the insurance companies, and for those who merely make small talk. And yet, even as these fronts pass over, even in the minute they leave these shores heading east, always east, they cease to be of interest, for the focus is always on the new and the next and yesterday's rain is lost forever, like a footprint in melting snow.

In South Africa, 'the weather' was a constant, brought to him from my earliest childhood to the last days of his life by the South African Broadcasting Corporation. Even now, I can repeat as a catechism the places on the map as the weather forecaster read the forecast, travelling from Cape Town to Durban, travelling east with the weather along that ragged coastline with its beaches and inlets, sea cliffs and wide expanses of golden sand and with its cities and harbours, their colonial names harking back to people and places, victories and defeats long forgotten by those who live there. Plettenberg Bay to Cape St Francis. Cape St Francis to Port Alfred. Port Alfred to Port St Johns. Port St Johns to Port Shepstone, onwards and eastwards, taking in the cities too, Port Elizabeth and East London, Algoa Bay even and then turning north to where we lived in Natal. The province of Natal, which extends from the Mtamvuma River in the south to the Mozambique border in the north and encompasses all of what for many years was known as 'Zululand', was so named by the Portuguese explorer Vasco da Gama who had left Lisbon in 1497, only five years after Columbus made landfall on Hispaniola. Da Gama was in search of a sea route to India and, on Christmas Day, was some way off the coast of what was to become South Africa. Here, with what I imagine to be a sweep of his arm, for he did it without bothering so much as to set foot on it, he named all the land visible from his deck Natal.

And the weather in Natal where Dad spent the second half of his life was itself always different and always the same. The long dry months of winter were punctuated only occasionally by forgiving soft mist, and the hot volatile days of summer in turn were disturbed by the afternoon thunderstorms which one could watch building and building. They would pass by in brief flurries of rage, washing the dusty African sky to leave the cleanest and brightest sunsets, which Dad would watch, his pipe in hand, from our house on the hill. He would not embark on the smallest chore, the repair of some guttering perhaps, or a trip to the library to return some books, without first listening to the weather forecast. This he would do in heroic mode, poised in silhouette beside the radio, his chin in a contemplative hand, his head slightly bowed. And nothing, as my mother later recalled, pleased him more than the idea of a little something, perhaps rain, preferably some 'murk' – how he loved his 'murk' – coming up the coast. Though, in truth, any sort of weather would do and one had a sense that the appeal of the forecast lay in just that: that momentary, elusive ability to see into the future, to read one's partner's cards and one's opponents' intentions and to dress accordingly.

But it was not only the predictive qualities of the weather forecast that pleased Dad, nor indeed did he always like what was coming. A bit of murk spoke, I believe, to the same heart that knew the 'haar', the sea mist that would sometimes sit on Edinburgh for days on end, a cold wind coming in from the Firth. But he disliked the heat and the dry 'Berg winds that would sweep down from the Drakensberg escarpment parching everything in their path. And I suspect that, in listening to the weather, he was really looking for precipitation, which he loved in all its forms. Hardly a man for all seasons, he was a man for the rain and the mist, for sleet and snow, and it was not the cold or the wet that appealed but its cleansing embrace. I can remember as a child lying in my bedroom, listening to the crash of hailstones on the corrugated roof, and wondering at the spectacular fury of those clouds, so white and soft and so distant, and yet so able to explode in flurries of rain and thunder and lightning. And it was not only the noise and the white light that split the heavens if the storm came after dark, but also the gushing water that ran off the roof and off the awnings and off the trees into the guttering and the paving and down the sides of the hill on which we lived, crashing through the undergrowth to the Gorge and the Emolweni River, which over millennia had cut this vast crevasse through the sandstone and from there eventually to the sea.

Even now I cannot hear the phrase 'Partly cloudy and hot with isolated thundershowers' without immediately calling Dad to mind. I see him in his chair by the radio, a book perched on his knees or thirteen cards dwarfed in his long gnarled hand as he surveyed the view from his window, or me or any of the other distractions that intruded on the thoughts of this most private and isolated of men. It is curious also to think too in this image summoned by the weather forecast how his body is neither young nor old, although in my mind it has certain characteristics of the later part of his life: it is folded up, all 6'5" of it, like a concertina, the edges worn from use but the notes still true and the melodies precise.

His knees are brown from the sun. They are conspicuously South African, demarcated exactly by the distance from the bottom of his short trousers to the top of his long socks, which he wore in the South African manner. Either side of these dividing lines, his skin was Scottish, pale and blue-veined, soft and bald, the hairs long since worn away by the friction of the cloth. But the knees themselves were of the colonies, knees that had seen action in North Africa and Italy, knees that knew the sun and knew the grazes and scabs that come from playing rugby on the hard winter fields of the Eastern Cape. These were knees that were, at least until his final days, dark and taut, as though stained with betel juice and preserved in tannin from the wattle trees that grew in abundance in Natal.

It was his knees, too, which caused excited comment some thirty-five years ago when we went *en famille* to Scotland, where in Edinburgh some children made fun of Tom both for wearing shorts and for the colour of his knees and were shocked to find themselves cussed in the roundest accents and ripest language of Fife. And I remember my father being surprised at himself, as it must have been fully thirty years before that he last spoke like that. But, now I think of it, as with his knees so with the rest of him too. Those parts which were not clothed, his head and his hands and forearms and a deep V about his neck, had been claimed by the sun, by Africa, by experience, but his heart remained in part in Scotland, in the mists and soft heathers (though, in truth, he was a city child) and in what I suspect always felt to him to be a state of comparative innocence, unspoiled by the long years of his exile or the war and unscarred by the natural vicissitudes and compromises of life. It was an innocence to which I suspect he often longed to return but he never believed he could. For it was axiomatic that there was no going back, not for love and certainly not for money. The water flows to the sea and stays there. The drop that fell in the High Street, Kirkcaldy, ended up beside the warm waters of the Indian Ocean. It mattered not one jot to him that it could have been otherwise.

It was his firm belief that the card once played, even the wrong card, must stay on the table as it does in bridge, a penalty card the playing of which one's opponents may determine at their leisure, which is to say at the moment when it may extract from your good self the greatest price. For, just as he loved its rules and their certainties, Dad loved the fact that bridge has no particular etiquette of sympathy and even the most brilliant players will be able to recount the intense, public and drawn-out humiliation of playing a mistakenly bid hand.

The moment the first card is led in a hand of bridge, dummy puts his cards on the table. There are twenty-five cards invisible to declarer, and yet for all the information that has been given in the bidding, and for all the ability of declarer to know his opponents and to guess the position of their cards, still it is easy to get it wrong. Declarer is peering always 'into a glass darkly', working with what he knows, guessing at the rest. But I am aware that, in insisting on the rules, which is to say that 'A card prematurely exposed (but not led) by a defender is a penalty card', Dad would unconsciously have made a transition in his mind. Just as he saw himself as declarer and not as dummy, so he saw himself not as the one who made the error and paid the penalty, but as the one who extracted the pain and determined the price. It was a transition that, though it was undoubtedly true of him at the card table, was not, I think, true of him in life.

26. A tour of duty

THE HEAT AT Durban airport is almost unbearable. David picks me up in his *bakkie*. We have, he says, less than half an hour to get to the hospital. Jackie's already there. She came in from Brussels and was able to catch the earlier connection from Johannesburg to Durban. We run for the car. As he drives too fast along Sydney Road, David explains that the operation to remove the cancerous blockage is set for ten o'clock that morning. Dad is very weak. He might not make it.

Nor might we, the way David is driving. We screech to a halt outside the hospital and rush in. The nurses recognise David; he knows his way and we hurry through to the wards. Despite the long night in the aeroplane, I realise I am unprepared for this.

The hospital corridor leads past the nurses' station. A series of doors lead off to the right. David nods at the third one. I knock and go in. It's a shared ward with five beds and huge windows overlooking Durban Bay. The room is bright and clean and pleasantly cool after the early-morning heat of midsummer. Jackie is standing near the door. We hug briefly and I look for Dad.

'Where is he?'

She looks at me for a moment and then nods at one of the beds. I glance at it and then look around again, but she points me back to the bed. It takes a moment to realise that this old man, this shrunken, whiskered shadow of a man, is my father. His eyes are closed against the light.

'He's very weak,' Jackie says. 'He hasn't eaten since yesterday because of the operation.'

At the sound of voices, Dad opens his eyes. I haven't changed and he recognises me immediately.

'You made it,' he says, though he hasn't the strength to smile.

'So will you,' I say.

He grunts. 'Och, well...' and he shrugs. 'Perhaps.'

'Are you afraid?'

He grins weakly and grunts again. 'Just bloody knackered,' he says, as his eyes close.

The nurses come to usher us out. It's time for the operation.

We go home to wait. The call comes a few hours later. The operation has been a success. He is alive. He will survive on a liquid diet for a few days; within a week, he should start taking solids. Yes, we should make preparations for him to come home.

But later, when we meet the physician, he qualifies this assessment. The operation has been a success insofar as it has cleared the obstruction to Dad's throat. But he has not tried – and sees no point in trying – to remove the cancer. To do so will surely kill Dad. Any care from now on will only be palliative. We can ease his pain; we cannot fix him.

In his ward, Dad looks, if possible, even smaller than he did that morning. He is grumpy and clearly in pain.

'You can go now,' he says. 'I never did like bloody kibitzers.'

His eyes are closed before the door.

But he did like an audience, which is not quite the same thing. At home we decide it is better to visit him in turn and we establish an informal rota. The next day, I have the morning shift. He seems glad to see me. We talk about a book which is about to be published and about my children. He asks the right questions – how is Cal? What are the girls up to? – but he is impatient with the answers. He seems to have something on his mind.

He looks about him furtively. 'So let me take you on a tour,' he says.

'Do I want to go?'

'Sure you do. How else do you learn anything?'

'Really?' I'm not sure I want this at all, but he seems determined.

'It'll be fun.'

I pull the curtains around his bed so we have privacy and help him to lift the sheets off so that he can show me what remains of his body. It is strange and distancing, which I imagine is as he intended, to see this muscle-free, bony old body. He has no penis – that 'went' with his cancerous bladder before Christmas. There is a great cut the whole way up his abdomen from the previous day's operation. On his side, there is another hole. This one has a tap for the colostomy bag. There is no muscle, no bulk, no strength. He looks like something laid out in a biology class. Feel here, he insists. Have a look at that. His body is a Technicolor dreamcoat of bruises that will never heal, but he seems to gather strength from the 'tour'.

'One day, my son,' he says, adopting the sonorous tones of a pompous captain of industry, 'all this will be yours.'

I appreciate the handover, but all I can manage is a weak smile.

'Hey,' he says, 'I'm the one who's bloody dying.'

The tour continues. His ribs are like the windblown dunes of a dry, white desert. 'Try this,' he says, and he shows me how if you pinch his skin it takes several minutes to resume its place.

His skin is cold and soft, and very pale.

'Are you ready?' I ask.

To some questions, there would appear to be no answer and I do not really expect him to say anything. It's his turn to smile weakly and then to look out the window.

'It's your lead,' he replies.

The day Dad died was like any other. It was 'shorter' for him and felt longer to us. He was seventy-six years of age, which was, as he put it, 'neither young nor old'. Alert until the last two days when a cocktail of morphine and gin enhanced his going, he seemed to me to have lived a life I knew only partially. It was not that I did not know some of the details, nor that I had not lived a life of comparable distraction. I had, after all, reversed his southbound journey by leaving South Africa to live in Britain. I too had three children. And I too sometimes find myself consumed by doubt as to the proper place of private action in public life. It was more that in his triumphant ordinariness – his strength and his weakness – my father posed questions that I was not always willing to accept. There was one particular afternoon in his hospital ward when we were struggling, as we had for some days, properly to time our goodbye. This time I wanted to remember it. We were watching a yellow-billed kite ride the thermal currents coming up from the Bay when he remarked on how stilted we were in our declarations of love, how incompetent at speaking from emotion. He said that he knew of no one – and forgive the proud father's hyperbole – better with words than he and I, and couldn't understand why we found it so difficult to say what must have been blindingly obvious to the silent patients watching us from the four other beds in the ward. I, choked with emotion, found little answer and, as was our way, we took refuge in the metaphor of bridge. I vaguely recall some banter about 'low raises' and 'forcing passes'. There may even have been something about 'doubling for takeout', a conversational gambit with which we were both familiar and in which the invitation to takeout was invariably accepted in an attempt to reach safer, less emotional ground.

Outside the window, the kite turned effortlessly on the self-replicating thermals, rising and falling. Dad took a breather from these conversational exertions by pulling on his ill-fitting oxygen mask, which then lay askew on his erratically whiskered face, giving him the appearance of a mildly deranged pirate. I stood at the window and watched the bird. Like any child of that part of South Africa, I could recognise it from below from the distinctive 'V' shape of its tail. But the hospital was perched on the edge of the high hills of the Berea and, from time to time, the kite would swoop below me. For the first time I recall, I was able to observe its colouring from above, and I remembered Melville's memorable passage in *Moby Dick* in which he wrote that there is 'a Catskill eagle in some souls that can alike dive down into the blackest gorges, and soar out of them and become invisible in the sunny spaces. And even if he flies forever within the gorge, that gorge is within the mountain, so that even in his lowest swoop, he is still higher than the other birds upon the plain, even though they soar.' I realised then as I realise now that to cast my father in so heroic a mould is to presume too much. He was strictly a bird of the plain even when he soared, as sometimes, fleetingly, he had at the bridge table.

On that hot and desolate day in Durban, I left the kite to its troubling vortex and turned from the window back to my now sleeping father. He seemed impossibly small in his bed, so small that it was not easy at first glance to distinguish which were his limbs and which were just the folds of the white hospital sheets. I stood a long while at that distance and watched him. I have no real recollection of how much time passed. Perhaps it was ten minutes. Perhaps an hour. Nor do I remember what I was thinking, except feeling acutely – but not saying – that to be alive is always and everywhere to be vulnerable in hearts.

27. For the record

IF THIS WERE a movie, it would fade to black. Instead, we move slowly about the old house, packing our bags and getting ready to go our various ways. David and I find ourselves looking in corners. We find pieces of Dad in forgotten drawers. Some business cards that must date from the 1970s. A short story typed out one finger at a time, unfinished. A letter that starts 'Dear Sand,' and gets no further. In the twenty years I had lived in Britain, he wrote to me only twice. I think for a moment it must be of recent vintage. Perhaps he had something to say? But David shakes his head. The writing is too legible. It must be old. In the dining room, we find Dad's old campaign medals from the war. The Africa Star. The Italy Service Medal. The George VI Medal. Later, I take them home with me, to London. When, some months after that, I show them to Cal, he turns them over in his hand.

'So he got these for fighting?' he asks.

I nod. 'Although he always denied he actually did any fighting. He said he was always too far from the front.'

'Do you believe him?'

Do I believe him? I think about it for a moment and decide I do. In the big things, I believe Dad. 'I don't think he enjoyed being a soldier,' I say. 'He hated the fighting. I think he saw things that were really quite horrible.'

But Cal has moved on already. 'I miss him, you know,' he says, like someone stumbling over the thought.

One medal – the African Star – is engraved with the simplest legend: T. Balfour. Actually not engraved, but stamped in an uneven line. You can sense the impatience of the engraver. One down; how many thousands to go?

In Dad's cupboard, David and I discover our old school ties, which have somehow survived untouched since 1979. Never worn but nor were they thrown away. We suppose they will be now.

In the carport, the old tools lie undisturbed. Against the walls and in the rafters is more 'unsorted rubbish' through which we wander 'pulling up interesting fragments which might fetch a price or come in handy'. There are pieces of timber rescued from some or other project – Dad was always a reluctant and impatient handyman – and put by, like a spare trump, for a day when they might 'come in useful'. The way back to the house takes us through a gate erected to keep the dogs in. It has a cowbell attached, the nearest Dad ever came to accepting the need for 'security' in these crime-fearing days. Even now the house is completely unprotected. No fences, no alarms, no guns. The old pellet gun was handed in to the police some years ago, during one of their periodic amnesties for unlicensed firearms.

We wander back inside. These are our last moments and we're not very sure what to do with them. I will return to London, Jackie to Brussels. David is heading off to the bush somewhere. In one sense at least, Mum wants to be alone. The past few weeks have been exhausting; she needs time and space to recuperate. Already she has plans to sell the old house and move somewhere smaller. Our flat crown tree will become someone else's tree. Its leaves, nurtured with Dad's ashes, will give their shade to others. It's the right thing to do, of course, but we find ourselves looking out past the crest of the hill to the distances on either side and saying nothing.

It's a couple of days after the funeral. The weather has turned unpleasantly hot, the worst of the midsummer days. It is humid too, but the promised thunderstorms never arrive. They remain, as we do, 'isolated'. The dogs disconsolately seek shade. That evening we gather again in the sitting room. Mum sits in her corner where she has always sat, but we find that the geography of it doesn't work any more. Dad's chair sits in the corner, a resounding reminder of just what it is we no longer have the energy to discuss. Beside it is his stool with an old pipe in the ashtray. I wonder what Mum will do with it. Throw it out too, I suppose.

'Come on,' says Jackie. 'Let's play.'

We all look to David.

'Oh, shit,' he says. 'Is this absolutely necessary?'

Our silence confirms his worst fears.

'I'll get the table,' he says.

Jackie and I look at each other.

'You can have him,' she says.

'Thanks a bunch.'

'Boys against girls,' says Mum with a brittle brightness. 'Just like…'

But she can't bring herself to finish the sentence because it is not like anything we have done before. This is new territory for all of us. The four of us have never been 'a four'. We have never previously played bridge together. Not once in forty years. But, on this oppressive summer night in Durban, with the barometer hovering in the danger zone and the neighbourhood dogs barking their frustration in endless rounds, David has little choice but to relent. It has become necessary for us to play bridge. And so this prolonged, tender and dismal vigil is the first time, and probably the last, that we four will play together.

Boys against girls. The pairings bring a slight – but false – edge to proceedings. Jackie teases David. I confine myself to the occasional foolish pre-empt. Mum plays mechanically. David and I are determined to follow Skid Simon's famous dictum, which comes to us by way of Dad: 'When in doubt, bid one more.' We do. Almost every hand we bid one more, and down we go. Sometimes a little and sometimes, as Dad used to put it, 'a lottle'. But we're pretty sure he would have been proud of us, for, though the 'girls' won, we lost with style. Or at least comprehensively.

And once, just once, we got it right:

NORTH

Me

♠ 10 6 4

♥ A

♦ A Q 5

♣ Q 9 8 5 4 3

WEST		EAST	
Mum		Jackie	
♠ A Q J 9 8 7 2		♠ K 5 3	
♥		♥ Q 2	
♦ K J 8 7		♦ 9 4 3	
♣ 7 2		♣ A K J 10 6	

SOUTH

David

♠

♥ K J 10 9 8 7 6 5 4 3

♦ 10 6 2

♣

They are spectacular hands. The bidding goes like this.

WEST	NORTH	EAST	SOUTH
Mum	Me	Jackie	David
1 ♠	2 ♣	Double	4 ♥[1]
4 ♠	5 ♣[2]	Double	Pass[3]
5 ♦[4]	Double[5]	5 ♠[6]	Pass
Pass	6 ♥[7]	All Pass[8]	

Dad seems to be watching. I can hear him whispering in my ear as the bidding progresses.

1. That's my boy. It didn't all go in one ear and out the other.

2. Why? Bid 6 ♥ . I hope David leaves you there. I hope Jackie doubles you. You'll go down a million and you deserve it.

3. Oh, dear. I didn't mean it about leaving you there! Well, you made your bed and now you can lie in it.

4. Oh, very clever, dear. (This comment is both genuine and sarcastic. 5 ♦ is an elegant but, under the circumstances, very unfortunate bid.)

5. Oi! Watch what you say to my wife.

6. Jackie always was the best bidder in the family. You could learn a thing or two from her. Mum's spades can't be that good if she's got diamonds as a second suit and in that case 6 ♠ is unlikely to make.

7. Better late than never. With any luck, someone'll double you.

8. Didn't they learn anything? Always bid one more. How many times do I have to say it? One down is good bridge. Well, it's cold now.

No one doubles and no one bids one more. David has bid the hearts and so he has to play the hand. Needless to say, if we had been left in 5 ♣, I might just, through good play, have managed to get out of it for seven down.

But a contract of 6 ♥ cannot fail. The contract is cold. There are no losing tricks in the black suits, for David can trump anything the opposition might lead. He has only to lead twice through West's diamonds (given her 5 ♦ bid, Mum is almost certain to have the king) to make two tricks in that suit. He does that successfully, runs his trumps and finally concedes a diamond trick. A small slam, bid and made.

David is elated. It's his first and only slam.

'You see,' I say, 'bridge can be fun.'

'The old man would have been proud,' he agrees.

'The "old man",' says Jackie, 'would have bid seven.'

For the first time in weeks my mother smiles.

Acknowledgements

There are many thousands of books on bridge, more than anyone could read. The authors that I found most helpful and to whose books I returned again and again are Victor Mollo, S.J. Simon, Alan Truscott, Rex Mackey, Terence Reece, John Clay and Zia Mahmood. And, of course, Ely Culbertson. In the course of writing this, I spoke to many world-class bridge players. All were unfailingly polite and helpful as I explained that I was writing a book about bridge that wasn't really about bridge at all. None asked why I was wasting their time. In particular, I would like to thank Alan Truscott, David Burn, Zia Mahmood, Fred Gitelman, Michael Rosenberg and Tatiana Ponomareva. My thanks too to my excellent editors, Toby Mundy and John Glusman, to Bonnie Chiang and Corinna Barsan, and to my friend and agent, Isobel Dixon.

My family suffered through many drafts of the book and were kind enough to say they enjoyed it.